THE ROAD TO SPLITSVILLE

How to navigate the road to divorce without making yourself crazy, your children miserable or your lawyer wealthy.... and then discover your path to happiness

By

Jeffrey S. Stephens, Esq.

and Ronald Raymond, PhD © 2022

A POST HILL PRESS BOOK

ISBN: 978-1-63758-809-3

ISBN (eBook): 978-1-63758-810-9

The Road to Splitsville:

How to Navigate the Road to Divorce without Making Yourself Crazy, Your Children Miserable or Your Lawyer Wealthy.... and Then Discover Your Path to Happiness

Post Hill Press

New York • Nashville

posthillpress.com

Published in the United States of America

1 2 3 4 5 6 7 8 9 10

DISCLAIMER

The contents of this book are not intended, nor should they be construed, as one-on-one legal advice or therapeutic treatment. We have no way of knowing the unique circumstances you face and we are therefore unable to give specific counsel or care. Our intent is to provide guidelines to assist as you go through a divorce by providing information that will support you in this process; to present brief, interactive questionnaires to illuminate the various issues you are likely to encounter; to suggest possible solutions to the problems posed by divorce; and to furnish instructions on how best to work your way along this journey.

Table of Contents

CHAPTER 1
BEGINNING THE JOURNEY

"It is better to light a candle than to curse the darkness"
Eleanor Roosevelt

Let's get this out of the way right up front—this book is not for people interested in saving their marriage. Actively trying to make your marriage work is something we wholeheartedly endorse—if you feel there is any chance you can restore and revive the feelings that led you to wed in the first place then run, do not walk, to find the best therapist available and try to work things out. Your marriage began as a sacred pledge, and it is not our intention to denigrate the importance of that bond.

However, as we will mention more than once in this book, the sad reality is that half the marriages in the United States end in divorce. We wish it were not so. We wish there were some magic we could use to help people fight through their problems and commit to their original vows, but that is not how our world works. We have become a disposable society, and that includes the nuclear family.

Trust and mutual respect are basic to the foundation of every human relationship, including friendships, interactions with colleagues at work and, of course, marriage. Issues will always arise between people, and the answer to whether you can work things out is dependent upon four key factors:

1. The commitment you have to that relationship.
2. The seriousness of the trouble that has arisen between you.
3. The degree to which the trust and respect have been compromised by what has occurred.
4. The amount of pain the relationship is causing.

Even in the best of marriages, when trust is betrayed, or the relationship is otherwise damaged, any chance the harm can be repaired will depend on the view you and your spouse have of these four elements. You will have to decide whether your marriage is worth whatever it takes to make things right, and there must be a sincere effort by both partners to take responsibility for what has occurred. Only from there can you rebuild the trust and respect you shared.

Since you are reading this book, we assume you have decided that these steps are not possible and that you want a divorce. Even so, you may still be engaged in an internal debate that centers around the question, "Am I making the right move?" Be assured, that reaction is normal when contemplating one of the largest steps you will ever take in life.

In our experience, with hundreds of people going through divorce, a review of the four factors we listed above have led them to conclude that the damage is too great to rectify and/or their spouse lacks the willingness to do the work necessary to repair the harm. Along the way they have doubts, questions and fears about this process—as you will. Again, that is to be expected. You may find yourself asking questions, such as, "How could I have been so foolish?" Or, "How could I have been so blind?" Or, "How could my spouse have done this to me?"

This book is intended to help you answer those questions as you navigate the path to divorce. It will also focus on the doubts, fears and other corrosive emotions that come with the territory. For instance, it is natural to wonder if you might have prevented the split had you been less trusting, less vulnerable, or even more suspicious. But is that the sort of marriage you deserve? We want to free you from that thinking and help you avoid the tendency to build an emotional wall around yourself as a defense for the future. Sealing yourself off from others in order to avoid further pain is a surefire way to hinder your chances for happy relationships going forward.

As already stated, this book is intended for people who have concluded that they are going to divorce. We hope to minimize the emotional and economic damage to you—and your children, if you are a parent. Pain is inherent in the fact that your marriage is being dissolved, there is no denying that, but it can be managed and minimized. We hope you will come to think of us as two advisors with a unique set of skills and knowledge, who want nothing more than to lessen the upset as we guide you through this process.

Throughout the book there are a few asterisks ("*") which are intended to direct you to the source of the information cited, which can be found at the end of the book.

You will find that this book is interactive on many levels. There are questionnaires and exercises designed to help you focus on various issues. You are going to be asked to participate in this process as we move along, and we believe you will be glad you did. There are also free links to an audible collection that will be helpful. We recommend you listen to the first download when starting the book, as it will help you find a state of general relaxation during this journey.

> ***DOWNLOAD #1*** *In order to help you relax as you begin, we suggest you listen to this audio offering at www.theroadtosplitsville.com and go to the link for Splitsville Download #1*

Along the way, we will share various stories of people we have worked with—of course the facts and names have been altered to protect their privacy. You will find these throughout the book in *italics*. We hope you can empathize with a lot of these couples, and perhaps find something of value in relating to what others on the road to Splitsville have experienced.

You are not the first or last to go through this. You are not alone.

Whether you are rich or poor or somewhere in between, if you are preparing to get divorced then this book is for you. We have decades of experience, one of us a renowned psychologist, the other an experienced attorney. You can have a look at our credentials at the end of the book, but be assured this is not some elaborate sales pitch—neither of us is accepting any new patients or clients.

Our purpose is to demystify this journey, simplify the expedition, minimize the emotional turmoil and expense, and have you reach the other side of this path without the scars so many suffer unnecessarily on the road to a new life.

CHAPTER 2
WHY ARE YOU GETTING DIVORCED?

"When we are no longer able to change a situation, we are challenged to change ourselves." — Viktor Frankl

As you warily eye the title of this chapter, you may be thinking, "I know exactly why I'm getting divorced. My spouse was a [*fill in the blank*]. Why do I need to waste time searching for an answer I already have?"

We understand that reaction, but there is more to your decision to divorce than the fact your partner was unfaithful, unloving, unreliable, abusive, a loser, or simply no longer compatible with your needs. You need to dive deeper than that for two critical reasons—first, by clearly identifying the mistakes in your marriage that led to your decision to divorce, it will be easier to deal with the emotional issues the process will inevitably evoke; and second, it will help you avoid making similar blunders in the future.

The purpose here is to illustrate the value of having a distinct understanding of *all* the factors that got you to this point. Be certain of this—you are about to embark on one of the toughest rites of passage anyone can face in life. It is critical for you to have a precise understanding of what led you to this expedition. We believe you will also come to see that an awareness of how you got here will help you to find happiness as you move on with your life.

As the saying goes, it takes two to tango, and divorce is almost always the work of both parties, rarely just the fault of one. Understanding your partner's flaws and taking responsibility for your own will make it much easier for you to negotiate this voyage. It will also serve you well when you search for your next significant other. Please do not rush through these sections in your eagerness to find answers about the mechanics of how to divorce. We promise that the information you find in this chapter will help you to deal with the process of splitting and to feel stronger and better about your decision.

So then, let's start with a basic proposition—even though it may be hard to recall right now, we have to assume that at some point you loved the person you married. Whatever happened to extinguish those flames, you should not forget why you took your vows in the first place. It will assist you in gaining a clear understanding of what has gotten you from there to here.

You may feel you already know why things didn't work out. You cheated on her, she cheated on you. He/she became a verbally abusive sonofabitch. She/he became a nag. Your sexual needs and preferences diverged or one of you stopped wanting to have any sex at all. He/she fell in love with someone else. He/she spends too much money. She/he is a cheapskate. His/her breath is rotten. Her/his parents dominate your life and he/she will not confront them. You never thought he/she was going to get this fat. She/he drinks too much. And on and on.

Whatever fits your situation, it is critical to understand that all of these are only symptoms of a deeper issue. We all have faults, but people in love overlook a lot when they feel supported and understood and valued for who they are. Couples who do not feel those positive things will overlook nothing. All of which raises the obvious question—What led to these problems in the first place? For instance, why did your spouse cheat? What caused you to betray your spouse's trust? Why are the two of you so angry? Uncommunicative? Destructive towards each other?

Things that seem simple on the surface rarely are.

Take a moment to consider some of those couples we are all familiar with, those pairings we simply cannot figure out. She's beautiful and he looks like a gargoyle. She's fat as a horse and he keeps himself in great shape. You find him dull as dishwater while she is as bright as a klieg light. Friends consider her boring but her husband is a hilarious story-teller. When you are out to dinner, he is a tightwad and she is as generous as can be. But somehow they seem to be devoted to each other and their marriage is intact.

How do they make it work?

They're in love, that's how. They share trust and respect. They support one another. They have a connection with their partner that you do not, at least not anymore.

Why?

Whatever has led to your decision to divorce, it will be incredibly helpful to your emotional and physical health for you to drill down and discover what really went wrong—especially your share of the blame. Be honest with yourself, have a good look, then later we will discuss what steps you can take to help you get over it. Remember, the format of this book is to view this as a journey, and we have just identified the first step along the way.

We would like you to think of this chapter as a sort of "due diligence." For instance, if you were considering the purchase of a local coffee shop franchise, you would want to know how their other stores are doing across the United States, and maybe even in foreign countries. You would investigate the franchisor. You would be interested in the sales records of the store you are intending to buy, and the supply and demand for the products the store sells. In a similar manner, now that you are ending your marriage and moving on to the next phase of your life, you need to review how you got from the wedding to a divorce.

For centuries, the importance of marriage and family were widely acknowledged, but much has changed in the past several decades. In 1960 seventy-two percent of American adults were married. Although the decline has been gradual, the marriage rate is now down to about sixty-two percent. The data also demonstrates that the average age for first marriages has increased significantly. In 1969 the average age for women was 20 and for men 23, while 50 years later the average numbers are approximately 28 for women and 30 for men. (U.S. Census Department, 2019)

Marriage was once considered the most legitimate way to be in a relationship, to have sex, and to have a family, but for many that is not true anymore. Add to that how easy it has become to obtain a divorce, and that "being a divorcee" is no longer stigmatized as it once was. Back in the day, every state required "cause" for you to obtain a divorce, and that could be messy. Infidelity, abuse, or abandonment were some of the typical predicates, and they could be difficult to prove. Today, almost every state has some form of no-fault divorce, meaning all you have to do is tell the court that you no longer want to be married and they will grant the decree—even if your spouse disagrees!

You are probably aware of how dramatically our society has changed when it comes to marriage and divorce. Whatever you think of the good and bad of all that, it should provide some comfort that you are not alone as you move along this bumpy path.

2.1 Tough as this may be, let's begin by taking a look back at your marriage.

As you move through your divorce and toward your new life, it will be incredibly helpful if you take some time to identify the qualities about which you and your partner were in synch from early on, and those where you experienced a disconnect. Examine how these things developed and changed over the course of time. Be honest about yourself and your spouse. This is not an attempt to ascribe blame—it's about recognizing the reasons why you fell in love in the first place and then fell out of love later. These factors are more primal than simply saying your partner is a cheater, an abuser, a neurotic, a drunk, a nag, or whatever. This is about the common needs and values that led to your original attachment and the differences that arose to drive the wedge between you.

In recent years, researchers have developed a way of understanding relationships they call "Attachment Theory" (Ainsworth and Bowlby). It refers to the emotional bond that explains how a relationship begins and is then sustained between two people. Attachment Theory began as a study of the child-parent relationship—the so-called "cradle to grave" phenomenon—but it was soon used to analyze the emotional bond that develops between adult romantic partners. It was found that the bond between infants and parents and the relationships between adult partners who "fall in love" share similar drives—a tendency to feel safe when the other is nearby; intimacy though physical contact; and the desire for communication in all its various forms. The more the parties share similar needs and means of satisfaction, the more likely the relationship will succeed.

So, you might ask, what does all this have to do with me and the hurt I am currently experiencing? You are reading this book to figure out how to get divorced, not to relive a failed experience with your partner, right?

Those questions are fair, but just stay with us. It will make sense.

Let us suppose your spouse was not much for discussions about feelings and emotions, but those things are important to you, something you consider a "must." Or your partner was comfortable with anger and arguing, while that sort of behavior makes you uncomfortable, even intimidated. Or you enjoy physical contact, everything from handholding to back rubs, but your partner was not inclined to overt displays of affection. Or your spouse tended to be clingy and dependent while you cherish your independence. How do you think any of those relationships are going to fare? What sort of issues can you imagine arose for those couples?

And how will this play out for them in the future?

To assist in this evaluation, here is a simple set of questions that relate to your various levels of attachment for "THEN" (back when your relationship was young and promising) and "NOW" (when things have become bad enough to end the marriage).

As with the other questionnaires in this book, please take your time, use a pen and a pad—or even better, a notebook you can keep—and really dig deep for these answers. Create two columns on the page, one for THEN and one for NOW, and then fill out the answers as suggested below. You will find the results interesting and illuminating.

SPOUSAL ATTACHMENT SURVEY

The purpose of this exercise is for you to rate your spouse on each dimension below, both THEN—when you first married—and NOW—as you prepare to divorce.

You may be surprised to find how this will assist in freeing you from the painful aspects of your marriage coming to an end. You will begin to forgive yourself—and perhaps allow some forgiveness for your spouse—all of which will help you heal and move ahead.

Do not feel limited by this list, you may come up with additional questions for which you should provide ratings and insights. The more you delve into these behavioral categories, the more you will see how you and your spouse first came together and how you have diverged over the course of time. In this process you will also learn a lot about yourself, which will help as you look for a new mate.

We ask that you rate each of these factors on a scale of 1-10, a rating of 1 meaning it is a serious problem area and 10 meaning that you feel completely satisfied in this area as it should be in a good marriage relationship. This is one of our interactive sessions, and we ask that you not skimp on the effort. Take your time in considering each of these questions. As we said, be sure you use a notebook and pad where you write out your answers. Please do not use a computer, actually write your responses out longhand—there are proven psychological reasons why this method is preferred. In addition to the numerical score, write a sentence or two describing those feelings in each category for both THEN and NOW:

My spouse's feelings toward me

My feelings toward my spouse

My spouse's feelings toward other loved ones (family, friends, children)

My spouse's reaction to my romantic advances

My reaction to my spouse's romantic advances

My spouse's reaction to my sexual advances

My reaction to my spouse's sexual advances

My spouse's need for freedom from me

My need for time away from my spouse

My spouse's willingness to engage in discussions with me regarding our relationship

My willingness to engage in discussions with my spouse about our relationship

How much my spouse cares about me compared to how much I care about my spouse

How much I care about my spouse compared with how much my spouse cares about me

My spouse's tendency to try and control our relationship

My desire to control the relationship

My spouse's tendency to criticize me

My tendency to criticize my spouse

My spouse's tendency to embarrass me in front of others

My tendency to embarrass my spouse in front of others

2.2 Why marriages fail

Now that you have engaged in this brief review and introspection, it is worth a few moments to understand why marriages fail. There are obviously any number of reasons, of course, but a study of divorced individuals (K. Kent, Journal of Marriage and Family) listed the following as the most commonly cited issues that led to their split, in order of frequency:

Infidelity

Constant arguing

Substance abuse

Domestic violence

Economic hardship

Lack of support from family members

Extraordinary situations

Do you recognize your marriage in some or any of those? Are there other problems not mentioned here that seem familiar? There is value in identifying what led you to embark on this path to Splitsville, since you are left to deal with the consequences.

The study mentioned above had a section where each divorced person was asked two simple questions. The first question was:

"Looking back at your divorce, do you ever wish that you had worked harder to save your marriage?" The overwhelming response to this was "No", that the spouse who sought the divorce thought they had given it all they had and could not have worked harder.

The second question was:

"Do you ever wish that your spouse had worked harder to save your marriage?"

Almost one hundred percent answered "Yes!" Although they wished their spouse had worked harder at changing the relationship, they felt there was nothing more they could or were willing to give to solve it.

The obvious conclusion is that these were people who had become convinced they needed to end their marriages. Since you have embarked on this journey with us, we assume you are one of them, and we suggest that it will be of value to confront the underlying problems you had and resolve them for yourself so you can move away from upset and make your way towards happiness.

Let's have a brief look at each of these categories:

1. Infidelity

The betrayal of infidelity obviously causes pain and an undermining of the basic trust that is the core of what makes a marriage work. The person you regarded as your confidant and most trusted partner has deceived you, leaving you to doubt yourself and the relationship. You may think, "Who is this person? How could they do this to me? Can I ever trust them or anyone again?"

For many couples, infidelity brings other issues in the marriage to the surface. Self-worth. Values. Rejection. Insecurities about your appearance, sexuality and attractiveness. Once these doubts arise, they can become as important as the infidelity itself.

If your spouse has cheated on you, it is totally normal for you to feel an aching sense of rejection. You may wonder if someone else can replace what has been lost. But you must come to accept that your spouse's cheating is not a reflection of you, and not a reason to question your own sense of self. It is their problem, they are the one who lacked faith and integrity, and you should never forget that.

For further insight into this issue, you may want to visit: www.womenshealthmag.com/relationships/a19906406/cheatingsurvey

Never blame yourself for the failings of your spouse.

Mary Ann, married to Neal for four years, decided it was a spring-cleaning day. Neal traveled a great deal for his job and was usually away from home three nights per week. Neal repeatedly maintained that his business preoccupied him and consumed most of his time. Since he was going to be away that night, Mary Ann thought it would be a great time to busy herself around the house.

She had never cleaned Neal's desk or tried to organize the mess there, but thought she would give it a try. She was soon shocked to find, in the back of his top left-hand drawer, buried under a pile of scrap paper, a receipt for a $1,500 necklace from a jeweler in New York City. She knew he had never given her anything like the description on the receipt and so she scrambled further through the drawer. She found three credit cards in the name of "Benjamin Torres", along with receipts for hotels and dining, all paid under that name.

The next day, when Neal returned, she confronted him with her discovery. Ashen-faced and with much stammering, she demanded an explanation. He claimed he had purchased the necklace for a friend to give to his wife for their anniversary. As for the credit cards, he said they were in that name because his company required it for some sort of tax purposes.

Mary Ann did not believe him, and felt a deep sense of betrayal, especially at the casual way he tried to explain all of this away. She knew Neal was lying and knew that all this evidence involved another woman. Then she made the mistake by beginning to blame herself.

"If only I had not gained these five pounds, if I had agreed to all the types of sex he wanted, if I had dressed up more often in sexy lingerie, then this probably would never have happened."

NO! NO! NO! Blaming yourself is not the answer. If there was any chance for the marriage to survive, NEAL HAD TO TAKE RESPONSIBILITY FOR HIS INFIDELITY. Even if any of the issues she mentioned in her "self-blame attack" were behind his infidelity, it was his responsibility to work on solving them in a constructive manner, to discuss them with her—not to CHEAT on her as a solution.

In the end, Neal would not admit the truth, but Mary Ann's further investigation revealed multiple calls on his cell phone, to and from a woman in New York City. Mary Ann divorced him and moved on with her life. This was several years ago, and she has since remarried and reports a deep trust and love between her and her new husband. It was not easy at first, but it began when she learned to stop blaming herself and value who she was!

2. Constant Arguing

Some people in contentious marriages actually come to believe that arguing is a natural interaction between partners. While debate and even disagreement can be healthy, constant arguing can become corrosive, especially if it includes personal insults and attacks. Endless bickering will drive a wedge between spouses until it may become impossible to repair the damage.

This is especially true when the arguments descend into criticism and contemptuous language. Does this sound familiar? If so, it is usually a symptom of a deeper dissatisfaction with the marriage, from one or both of you. It is extremely difficult to support a relationship when you constantly feel you are under siege, being judged and put down by the person who is supposed to provide your most important support system.

3. Substance Abuse and Addiction

Dealing with a partner who is wrestling with alcoholism, narcotics or some other form of addiction requires an entire book of its own, so we will keep this simple. If you have had to confront this, you already know all the buzz words. Tough love. Enabler. Co-dependent. And so on.

You realize, in your heart, whether you have done all you are capable of doing to help your spouse deal with their problem. You are aware, in your soul, when it is time to move on.

Addictions range from alcohol to sex to opioids to gambling or even an inordinate amount of time devoted to work. There is no question that addictions can hijack your partner's ability to participate in a healthy and happy relationship with you. At some point, if your partner is not getting the help they need and working to subdue their demons, the best thing for both of you is to say, "enough is enough" and gather up the courage to divorce.

<u>Sometimes the lying is worse than the addiction.</u>

Murray swore to Jeannie that he was "absolutely done with drinking." He attended AA two nights per week and she went to Al-Anon on the same nights. Jeannie felt a deep sense of forgiveness for the pain Murray's alcoholism had caused them in their six years of marriage.

One night, during a winter snowstorm, the electrical power went out, and Jeannie began to light the fireplace. When Murray heard was she was doing from the adjoining room he began yelling at her for not asking him before trying to light a fire. He ran into the room, reached up into the chimney space and retrieved three bottles of vodka he had taped there. One of them was nearly empty.

Jeannie began to recall the evenings when Murray fell asleep early while they sat together in the family room. And other nights when she would go to bed and he would claim he had something to do downstairs, then later climb into bed and lay with his back towards her so she was unable to see or speak to him. Jeannie realized that she had begun trusting him again, but that she was being duped. He did not give up alcohol, had lied about going to AA, and she decided then and there that the relationship was over. With all sense of trust gone, she knew her only path was to Splitsville.

Addictions can be the reason for divorce, but sometimes it is not just opioids, alcohol, gambling, or other compulsions. Sometimes, as with infidelity, the betrayal of trust is the larger issue.

There is no question that addiction itself can destroy a marriage, but there is also the way these dependencies can hijack your partner's integrity when the substance abuse becomes a much higher priority than their commitment to a good and happy relationship with you. If you have been living with an addicted spouse who refuses to get professional help, you become as much a victim of their problems as they are. The best way to help yourself and your spouse, is for you to gather up the courage to divorce and move on with your life.

4. Domestic Violence

Domestic violence occurs all too frequently and is too often misunderstood. One of its most important aspects is that it does not always entail physical attacks. Domestic violence is any pattern of abusive behavior in a marital relationship that is used by one member of the marriage to gain or maintain power over the other. This includes repeated humiliation, incipient manipulation, intimidation, severe rejection resulting in deep feelings of isolation, creating an environment of fear of harm, repeated blaming without cause, coercion, and of course physical assault. This list is intended to encompass emotional, sexual, economic, and spiritual types of abuse. Hopefully you have not experienced any physical violence, but you may have suffered name-calling, extreme possessiveness, controlling behavior, distrust, or outright threats. All of these are types of abuse.

It is apparent that none of the conduct outlined above is going to allow for a successful marriage. Too often, the victim of abuse believes they are somehow responsible, at least in part, for this dysfunctional situation. Even if that is true, it is no reason to endure the pain. If you were standing on a train track and a locomotive was bearing down on you, you would not remain there simply because that was where someone had placed you. You would move on and save yourself. Enough said.

If you feel you are still in harm's way, be sure to consult with an attorney and/or local authorities to obtain appropriate protection.

<u>Abuse comes in all shapes and sizes</u>

Richard is undeniably a handsome man, Patti is an attractive woman, and the way they met is worthy of a cinematic rom-com.

Richard was skiing with friends in Aspen, took a bad fall, and ended up unconscious in the local emergency room where Patti was the attending physician. He suffered a concussion and a broken leg. His recovery was long and painful, and Fanny watched over him all along the way.

By the time he was released, their connection had graduated from friendship to passion. She was a few years older than he, and much farther along on her career path, but she moved back east with him, where he was preparing to enter business school with an eye toward becoming a hedge fund trader. Patti took a position in a local hospital, they set up house together and she supported him through school. Somewhere along the way they married. And then things went wrong.

We know what you're thinking, and you're right. You saw it coming, right from the top of the ski slope. So why didn't she?

Her awareness came in small steps, such as when he told her for the first time that he never wanted to have children. When was he going to mention that? Then there was the use of her savings, not just for household expenses, but for the harebrained schemes he came up with as he began a job and made some ill-advised investments. It turns out that Richard was not as smart as he was good-looking.

But Patti still loved him and believed that marriage was a forever arrangement. At least until he started cheating on her. Richard began treating her like the hired help, ignoring her feelings, the hurt and humiliation he was causing, yet all the while she paid for their home and food and made up for the losses he incurred as he moved from one company to the next.

Patti kept her chin up, a dangerous position with a potentially abusive spouse. She wanted to believe things would get better, but they did not. And then, irony of ironies, he told her that *he* wanted a divorce, having identified a new victim who had a bit more money and a few less years.

Patti is a brilliant, talented, loving person who simply could not understand any of it. How could he treat her this way? Why would he treat her this way?

She eventually discovered he had mortgaged their house to the hilt, had lost his latest position, left them effectively bankrupt, and was moving out. As wrong as everything was, she insisted that she had hung in there because she was still in love with him.

But was she really? Or was she unwilling or unable to admit her own mistakes, her failure to see what was real and what was not.

One of the points we want to make is that *abuse* comes in many different guises. The garden-variety abuse we generally think of is where a husband physically violates his wife—often with the encouragement of alcohol, as if meanness and stupidity were not enough. But there is a subtle form of verbal abuse that can injure a mate like the death of a thousand cuts. Put-downs, insults, criticisms that seem never-ending can not only rob someone of happiness, but it can also damage the ego and a person's sense of self-worth. And there are many other forms as well. Failing to engage emotionally with a spouse. Withholding sex. Cheating. Spending too much time with friends or at work while ignoring a spouse's needs.

In Patti's situation, we have a woman of great talent, accomplishments, and beauty— both physically and spiritually. We are therefore happy to report that she divorced Richard, found true love with a wonderful man and is now in the process of rebuilding, not only her life but herself.

As we will keep reminding you, there are many varieties of bad marriages, but that does not mean that your divorce cannot have a happy ending. How things turn out will be almost entirely up to you.

<u>Be honest with yourself about what is going on</u>

Irene Sellers, walked into the office for her therapy session wearing a raincoat that bore evidence of having been caught in the deluge outside. Despite four large windows and overhead lighting, the room was dark.

Irene's entrance was rather abrupt, and she was eager to dispel with the usual greetings.

When she dropped down in the large blue recliner, she made sure her coat, which remained buttoned up to her neck, also covered her legs. She began speaking in a rapid-fire manner, discussing her last session, when she reviewed the history of her marriage, claiming the exercise was interesting but useless. The simple fact, she said, was that she could not live with her husband any longer.

There was a red welt on her right cheek which she had tried to conceal with makeup, and when asked if she would like to share what happened to produce that mark, the question seemed to deflate all her aggression.

"Things have not been good," she said. "Reliving my marriage during the last session actually brought up a lot of upsetting memories for me. Especially about why I got married. I've spent hours this past week thinking about that." She managed a sad smile.

"Both of my parents are still alive. They've been married for over forty years. I have a younger brother, and he's been happily married for more than ten years. I can still remember how difficult it was for me at his wedding. I was twenty-six and I was alone. He was getting married and I wanted to be with someone. That's when I met Peter and thought I had fallen in love. But now, looking back, I realize it was really about my need to fall in love, my need to get married. It served my picture of how my life should be, to have a husband, and children and, maybe most important, to make sex legitimate." She paused before going on. "I came from a very conservative background. You can even say prudish. When I started dating Peter, I was uncomfortable about the way he pushed the issue of sex. It was important for him, and I knew that if I didn't give in, I would lose him." She

hesitated again. "This past week I spent a lot of time recalling my childhood. My brother and I were close and my parents were loving people. I realize now how much I wanted to duplicate that for my own children and how I hoped Peter would be a partner in all that."

Irene had already been told that studies indicate the prospect of having and raising children is a motivator for over forty percent of people getting married.

"Not much comfort there for a bad decision," she said. "The more I thought about it this week, the more I realized the bigger factor was my fear of ending up alone. Not really a good reason to get married, right? I thought that if I let Peter go, I might never find anyone else. And you don't have to tell me that was a ridiculous thought. Looking back, I know how wrong I was. But I gave in to him about everything, especially sex. I was an absolute fool, losing who I was in the hope of finding a long-lasting relationship, and now I discover I'm married to a sociopath."

She revealed things about Peter's violent sexual demands and increasingly abusive behavior she had never shared with anyone before, which returned her to the mark on her face. "He came home about three in the morning last night, drunk, and I could tell he had been with another woman. I've discovered he sometimes picks up whores at bars before coming home in the middle of the night. Last night I told him I knew what he was doing. He said nothing, he just slapped me across the face. Then he went downstairs, and I know he drank most of a bottle of his whisky, because he couldn't get back up to our bedroom. I'm ashamed to admit this, but other nights he would come in drunk, get into bed and essentially rape me."

After some discussion about how she had gotten from a hopeful bride to a victim of her own needs, she said, "It's time for me to get a divorce."

Irene's decision was not an easy one, involving major life changes, financial concerns, and the end of some of her dreams. But understanding how and why she had married was critical to her finding the strength to move on to build a new life. She was honest with herself, and that was how she found her freedom.

We want *you* to carefully examine how you got to this point. It will help you deal with the emotional strains along the way and will enable you to find the path toward your happiness.

5. Economic Hardship

Financial stress places a huge burden on both parties in a marriage, and for many it is an unfortunate fact of life. Money pressures often create a variety of hostile, irritable reactions between partners, and there is no easy fix when your checking account is tapped out.

Whatever your circumstances, there is a basic truth—partners who love, respect, and support each other will find a way to work things out together. For those who cannot find that common ground, the money problems become a symptom of an underlying flaw in the relationship itself.

There are literally millions of couples with little or no resources who make their marriages work, and an endless roster of wealthy people who divorce. The point is, if you and your spouse have let money destroy your marriage, then it was already a lousy match.

<u>Selfish is as selfish does.</u>

Gloria came to the realization that her spouse's practice of withholding money from her and asking her to account for every penny she spent was a destructive form of control. She then learned he was borrowing money each month from his parents and never paid it back. She began to examine their finances and found that he was running up debt on their credit cards, spending on unnecessary hunting equipment and other items intended for his pleasure alone.

When she finally had enough, she told him she was going back to work, but he insisted that was unacceptable, that she was a housewife and he was the provider.

Gloria found a job, saved what she could in a short time, and moved out.

Financial issues in and of themselves should not lead to divorce in a strong marriage, but they can often betray the weaknesses in a bad relationship and cause the ultimate split. Always be honest with yourself of what is going on, and never sell yourself short!

6. Lack of support from family members

We do not get to choose our families, and they do not get to choose who we marry. We all have relatives who disapprove of us, our friends, or our spouse—you know the story. If things go bad in your marriage, chances for the relationship to survive will in some part depend on the support system, and the critical commentary, from those around us.

Disapproving parents or siblings can place additional pressure on a marriage that should not exist, but it happens. The bond between partners has to be strong to deal with that sort of pressure and, if things are going bad between you and your spouse, this will only make it worse.

That is not to say we advocate taking a straw poll from those around you as you assess the health of your marriage. Just be mindful of who is important in your life and who loves you without reservation or agenda. Those are the people you should be listening to when things go wrong.

7. Extraordinary situations

There are any number of unusual marital occurrences, and these can be the most difficult to negotiate as one member of the marriage decides that divorce is the best decision for all. The following is just one example.

<u>The unavoidable ravages of time and health.</u>

Jan married Truman five years ago. She is forty years old now and he is sixty-two. It is the second marriage for both. Jan wed Truman out of a great sense of love and found him to be a deeply empathic and compassionate person. He was wealthy, an architect who had built and then recently sold a construction-based business for a considerable sum of money. Jan was a leading marketing manager for one of the largest department store chains in the country, earned a substantial salary and had a good deal of money saved herself.

The marriage was a true delight for both of them until one day Jan received a notice from an attorney advising that she had been put on a very limited spending budget since Truman had transferred all of their money to an account exclusively under his name. That night Jan tried to discuss the issue with him, but he refused. All he would say is that he had made out a new will that excluded her from any inheritance.

Truman's speech pattern seemed odd to Jan. He was speaking with a slight stutter in an unusually high-pitched tone. At times he did not seem to be making any sense and repeated himself over and over again. She was convinced there was something cognitively wrong with him, but when she asked how he was feeling he refused to answer.

Three days later, she found that Truman had booked a trip, just for himself, to a Club Med in the tropics. Going without her was completely out of character but he never mentioned it to her. Truman had stopped reading, canceled all his tennis dates, and refused to eat anything she made for dinner. Jan insisted he see a doctor, and although he resisted, she finally convinced him to go. After a series of tests were run, Truman was diagnosed with an aggressive form of Alzheimer's disease.

Jan was suddenly faced with a decision that would affect the rest of her life. All the physicians involved recommended that Truman be placed in a nursing home. Jan was still in her forties, attractive and bright with a great career, and she believed she could find a happy life for herself and maybe find a new relationship. Jan was heartbroken about Truman, but she felt that going on with her life was exactly what Truman would want for her.

Jan had to deal with a wide array of emotions. Guilt over placing Truman in a home. Concern over his well-being. The fear that she was being selfish. The worry about what the rest of her life would look like, how this would affect her career and how it would impact her prospects for a new relationship.

Jan, after much counseling, reasoned that this type of extraordinary stress must end in a divorce, even though she would make a continuing commitment to be there for Truman and his needs. As it happened, Truman deteriorated quickly and passed away just a couple of years after the onset of his dementia.

This was all extremely painful for Jan. However, she saw to it that Truman was well cared for throughout the remainder of his life. Now, a year since he passed, Jan is involved in a new relationship, with a man closer to her own age, who is intellectually and financially on the same level and with whom she has seemingly found a route to happiness, never discarding all of the wonderful things she experienced with Truman.

Marriage vows speak of a commitment for better or worse, sickness and health but, in some situations, it is important to allow for the need to move on.

2.3 How money issues can destroy a marriage

Money can take on many different roles in a marriage and can have many different effects. A wealthy spouse can use her or his position to control things. A spendthrift can create financial pressure in the relationship. Something as simple as disparate spending habits can result in all sorts of dissension. Here I will share the stories of two parallel cases, to give an idea how bad things really can become.

Trust and money

Diane is a delightful and trusting person. From the moment I met her, right up till today, we have been friends, and it was my privilege to represent her. She is bright and caring, does all sorts of charity work and the type of person who will be there for you if you need her.

Her husband was another story. Paul is a complete fraud. A liar. A philanderer. And, it turned out, an embezzler.

Diane thought they had a good marriage. Two lovely children. A nice home. A vibrant social life. And then one day it all came crashing down.

Diane had been out to the supermarket, her son and daughter in school, when she returned home and found a notice of foreclosure taped to the front door. She immediately called Paul.

In typical fashion, he lied. She learned over time that it was the one thing he did well. He assured her it was all a mistake. He was in the midst of refinancing their house, and this was nothing more than some technical mistake. Everything was fine, he told her. She demanded to know how he had begun a refinance without even mentioning it to her, but he made some demeaning remark about how she would not understand how the change in interest rates had made this a sensible move.

Sensible, she wondered? If it was sensible, why had he not discussed it with her? And how could a bank make such a drastic error, starting a foreclosure action this way?

But her nightmare was just beginning.

Diane called her bank to find out for herself what was going on. She was even prepared to criticize the officer there, whom she had known for years, until he began by apologizing. He said he had been expecting her call. He wanted to call her himself, but the bank's attorneys said it would not be appropriate, not with this lawsuit being filed. He told her that he felt horrible that she was in this position.

His words and tone made it evident that her problems extended beyond the foreclosure. She explained how Paul told her this was all the result of a clerical blunder caused by his application to refinance.

The bank officer was silent for few moments, until he finally said, "Diane, there is no refinance. Hasn't Paul told you about what's going on?"

He had not, she told him.

It was clear to Diane how painful it was for this man to speak with her, especially since he had been warned not to have the conversation. But he had known her for a long time and asked that she never divulge that any of this came from him.

"You have my word," she promised him, and he knew she would keep her promise.

He told her that the foreclosure was the unavoidable conclusion of a series of problems about which she knew nothing. Paul had been caught embezzling money from the company where he worked and had been fired. The mortgage payments on their home had not been paid for more than a year. Their savings account had been wiped out and Paul was facing serious criminal charges.

What the man did not tell Diane, but we discovered later, was that Paul had transferred large sums to a woman he had worked with, and whom he was "keeping" in an apartment in New York City. Almost all of those funds were also gone, and the other woman was also being charged, as Paul's co-conspirator.

As with other cases described in this book, Diane's first reaction was predictable—How could I not have known? What did I miss? How could I have been such a fool?

But Diane had trusted and respected her husband which, as we have also said, is the lynchpin of any solid relationship. How could she have known he was a liar and a thief and was only pretending to reciprocate those feelings?

Diane was a mother and a housewife who, as mentioned, did a lot of charity work. Paul handled all the finances. He regularly went through the mail before she saw it. He explained away any strange phone calls or odd-looking notices she may have seen.

Because She TRUSTED HIM.

The moral of the story is not to deride trust or to encourage people to live suspicious lives. The point is to be honest with yourself. When you see warning signs, no matter how slight, heed them.

In the end, Diane learned they were dead broke. We did the best we could to salvage something for Diane and her children as Paul went to jail. The house was sold at a public auction, but as an innocent spouse who had no part in her husband's misdeeds, the court allowed her to collect some of the equity from the sale. She divorced Paul, went back to work after years at home, and is doing quite well.

Another example

In a sort of reversal of roles, there was Elliot. Hard working, loyal and essentially decent. His wife, Noreen, was a spending machine.

She would splurge on clothing, for herself and their three children. She would continually redecorate areas of the home. She would spend time online, buying things they did not need. But Elliot loved his family and did his best, earning just enough so the income could keep up with the outgo. One day Elliot came home from work and tripped over several pieces of wood in the entrance to the bedroom. Staring up at him was a sauna unit to be installed by the contractors Noreen had hired. The unit had a price tag of $4,000 tacked to it.

He called down to Noreen, "What the hell is this?" He heard her laugh and then yell back that she felt they needed one because the neighbors next door just had one installed. Elliot stood in shock, thinking about how they were having difficulty paying the basic bills of living, and his wife thought nothing of this extravagance.

But Elliot did not tell Noreen to send it back, did not confront her about never even discussing the purchase with him, and simply accepted that he was going to have to figure out how to pay for it.

Once again, this was a situation where one of the spouses did not have the full picture.

When spending alone did not fill whatever emotional void Noreen was dealing with, as time went by in the marriage, Noreen took up gambling.

She played the stock market, options trading, even sports betting. In the end, they wound up where Diane found herself in our other example—bankrupt

The reason for sharing these stories is not just to illustrate how bad things can become when a spouse is out of control with finances. It is also important for you to know that both Diane and Elliot found new lives for themselves. They worked through the economic upheaval and learned ways not to blame themselves.

Could they have been more alert to what was happening? Should they have been? When you are aboard a sinking ship, is it more important for you to figure out what caused the leak or to find a way to get safely to shore? Should you go on berating yourself for the mistakes you made—real or imagined—and allow yourself to drown? Or should you look for ways to survive? Should you be searching for someone to blame, including yourself, or should you be looking for a lifeboat, a life preserver, a friend who can help you swim to safety?

The answers to all these questions should be obvious, but the important thing is how YOU answer them for yourself.

2.4 What if the problem turned out to be me?

Sarah is extremely attractive, reasonably bright, and undeniably sexy. It is not surprising, therefore, that she has little trouble attracting a mate. What is surprising is that she has already been divorced four times.

Most people count themselves fortunate to find one partner, or perhaps two if the first did not work out. But going to the proverbial altar for a fourth time takes a lot of nerve, and Sarah was in no short supply of that.

I represented her in divorce number two and helped shepherd her through the third and fourth because by then she lived in other states and needed to obtain local counsel. What I found remarkable about Sarah is her unwillingness to never own any of the blame for the failure of these four unions. As we advise in this book, after any divorce you should have a good look at what went wrong. That is, after all, the purpose of this chapter. But let's be real, when someone ends up with more divorces than winter coats, that should be a fairly strong signal that they need to examine the common elements of these debacles and figure out what adjustments might be made.

Not Sarah. Although she cheated on her first husband, she felt it was appropriate because he had become overbearing, boring, and uninterested in her—none of which was her fault. She cheated on her second husband because he had become critical, demanding and generally unpleasant—once again, she saw all of this as his doing and her infidelity consequently justified. In a twist of fate, her third husband ran off with their cleaning lady, which upset Sarah greatly, but which she ultimately ascribed to the fact that he was beneath her, as she told me—socially, financially, and intellectually. She felt that the fourth in her line of grooms was a nice enough man, but after ten tedious years she had no choice but to leave him or to fall into some sort of marital coma.

As we encourage you to take a tough, truthful look at why your relationship fell apart, we offer Sarah's case not to mock her unhappiness, but to make a point. At no time was she willing to examine why marriage after marriage failed. It was never her fault. It was always about the flaws of her mate. The results were not just emotional damage, but financial issues, difficulty with her children, and the various times she was uprooted from the lives she had built. All of which continues to lead her to to an inexorable result—she is doomed to keep repeating the same mistakes.

That is precisely what we do not want for you.

The most remarkable part of Sarah's story may not be the four divorces, but the other affairs that came and went along the way. You do not need to be married to destroy a relationship, especially if you follow a pattern destined to lead to disaster every time. The only way to avoid that is to do the difficult work of digging deep into your own situation so that you avoid driving into those same potholes again and again.

Sarah, ever the optimist, is now in her sixties and living with yet another man, with whom she reports to be experiencing another unfulfilling relationship. I expect to soon receive an invitation to her fifth wedding, ultimately to be followed by news of another divorce.

No matter how much you feel you love someone, marriage cannot fix the problems within yourself or fill a void that you feel, which only you can address.

2.5 Now take time to honestly analyze the reasons you have decided to divorce.

The decision to divorce should raise any number of questions you are asking yourself about how this happened. We would like to suggest a few to help you focus. Once again, we ask that you take your time and write out your answers, no matter how brief. You will find some of these questions quite straightforward, while others require personal insights and evaluations. Do those in a stream-of consciousness manner, don't judge or overthink things, just set down whatever comes to mind in response to each question:

QUESTIONNAIRE

1. What do you recall as the most prominent reasons you married? List them all.
2. How old were each of you at time of your wedding?
3. What jobs did you and your spouse have at that time and what do each of you do now?
4. Did you have any doubts about your choice back then and, if so, list each of them?
5. What have you discovered about your spouse in the course of your marriage that, if you had known back then, would have persuaded you not to marry?

6. In what significant ways (e.g., emotionally, physically, in terms of personality) has your spouse changed since your wedding day, whether for good or bad?
7. In what significant ways (e.g., emotionally, physically, in terms of personality) have you changed since your wedding day, whether for good or bad?
8. Looking back at your marriage, what do you wish your spouse had done differently?
9. Looking back at your marriage, what do you wish you had done differently?
10. What are the mistakes you believe you made in your marriage, that you are committed not to repeat in your next relationship.

You may have noticed that none of these questions relate directly to children, which we will deal with in a later chapter. The key here is to come clean about the relationship you had with your spouse. Be brutally honest, assess the good and the bad for two very obvious reasons we have mentioned before—First, it is imperative that you have a clear understanding of why you are leaving your marriage, which will help you deal with all aspects of that choice. Second, we do not want you to make the same mistakes again!

The following are examples of how three people, Allyson, Walter, and Cornelia, filled out this form. We include these because many of the participants who have completed the questionnaire include similar information. Perhaps you will find something of yourself here.

Allyson's Responses

1. I got married because I thought Clarence would make me the most important thing in his life. As a Christian, I also married to make it acceptable to have sex and to have a family.
2. I was 24 when we married. I was working for two years after graduating from college and hated my job. I thought if I married, I could quit my job and Clarence would support our family.
3. Clarence was a real estate agent when we met. I stopped working as soon as we got married and he continues to be a real estate agent.
4. I hate to admit it, but I had some doubts before we married that I did not honestly address. One of the biggest issues for me was the way he always seemed to be pointing out the sexy appearance of other women. When I told him it embarrassed me, he would claim that all men do that and refused to stop, saying it was my problem. As another example, after attending a party together, he would talk about how so and so looked at him with "sex on her mind," as if I should not be troubled by that.
5. This is closely connected, if not the same, as item 4, above. I should have recognized him as a womanizer even before we were married. Maybe I thought he would change, but I realize now he was cheating on me both before and after.
6. I don't think he changed much, especially when it comes to cheating on me. He was an unfaithful man before we got married and still is.
7. I've become more aware of Clarence's behavior. I am no longer as naïve or accepting as I was. I suppose the big difference is that I will not tolerate the cheating and I am getting stronger and more assertive in dealing with him. I stopped having sex with him because I knew he had been with other women and I don't want to risk getting an STD. I don't even see him as a person anymore, I see him as an animal.

8. This one is simple for me because I had come to accept that I should have listened to my doubting voices before I married. The questions were there, but I wanted to get married, so I overlooked them. I took our vows seriously, but obviously he did not.
9. I also wish I had faced the reality of the situation and put my foot down right from the start, or at least decided to get divorced earlier. I tried more than once to convince him that we needed counseling, but Clarence refused.
10. This one is hard, because at this point, I cannot imagine wanting another relationship. However, if it happens, I will pay attention to any signs of selfishness like the ones Clarence showed, especially of potential infidelity.

As it turned out, Allyson was able to create a new relationship that worked for her. She was able to use this questionnaire as a guideline in forming this new, healthy, intimate relationship. Her responses helped her confront the need to be truly appreciated. She realized that she overlooked signals that should have warned her that her ex-husband was too egocentric to love her as she deserved to be loved. Allyson related to us that the above questionnaire "opened her eyes to what was really important to her in forming a new relationship."

Walter's Responses

1. I got married because I was living alone, had a hell of a time keeping my apartment in any semblance of order or cleanliness, and I found Carla to be exactly the opposite. She held out the promise of resolving all the disorganization in my life. I never had any guidance or skill training from my very neglectful mother. I knew my life would be better with Carla than me alone.

2. I was 23 when we married. I did not have much experience with women before Carla and my relationship with her was like suddenly finding the mother who basically abandoned me when I was five and sent me to live with an elderly grandmother, who died when I was eight. I was placed with an adoption agency but never adopted. Carla was 27 and like me, had never been in an intimate relationship before we hooked up.

3. I graduated from high school but never went to college. I was a manager of a McDonald's. As a manager, I made a decent living, and the benefits were great and would easily cover us. Carla had been through college and was employed as an executive secretary at the Clorox Company.

4. I didn't have any doubts about marrying Carla. She seemed like the ideal partner for me. I figured she would move up even further in the company and I thought I might someday get to Corporate McDonalds.

5. I found that within the first year, Carla began to show a different direction than I had and that was annoying to me. Her understanding of the news and the political issues going on were well below my intellectual level and more like that of an immature child. She did not read, and I started to realize that we really had little in common.

6. I think the best way I can put this is that Carla became less caring for me and I no longer felt love from her or for her.

7. I have changed in a major way. I feel attracted to other women who represent more than just a sexual relationship possibility. I have lost the extreme level of sexual interest I had in Carla prior to marriage. I'm still sexually driven but in a much more mature way than I was with Carla.
8. I don't blame Carla for any of this marriage failure. I realize it's wrong to marry in the hope of getting someone who will take care of you.
9. I wish I had been more mature in the way I made the decision that she was the life-long partner I needed.
10. In my next relationship, and I intend to have one, I will pay attention to the important features of commonality between us, like interests, intellectual level and maturity. Sex, of course will remain important, but it will not be the determining force.

Over the ensuing four years, Walter was not able to sustain a relationship because he did not really understand himself. After a series of failed relationships, we met and had him re-read his responses to the above questionnaire. He admitted that in each case the woman who left him said that she knew it would never work out because he was too dependent. After a thorough review of his responses above, he had an "Aha" moment, coming to terms with the reality that he was looking for a mother not a wife. Walter decided to restart therapy with a new counselor. When we last spoke, he seemed to be profiting from those sessions and felt he is finally looking for a mate for the right reasons.

Cornelia's Responses

1. I got married because it fit the blueprint that matched what I wanted and what I thought my family expected of me. I also admit, I really thought he loved me.

2. I was 27 and Tad was 29. I recall my father saying that any woman who has not married by the time she reaches 27 is an old maid. Now that I am looking inside myself, I think I got married because I thought Tad was my last chance and I would not find anyone after him. I realize now that I knew he was not perfect, but I think I thought "Beggars can't be choosy."

3. I was employed as a librarian in the New Jersey State system and Tad was a landscaper. I thought he would soon own his own landscaping business. He is skilled but it turned out that he did not have any motivation.

4. I had no doubts at the time. I realize now, I was not examining things carefully enough. It is easy to look back and realize the concerns I should have had back then, especially about his lack of ambition. I believed he would get motivated to start his own business after we married, and especially if we had children. I was even wrong about that part, because I only discovered later that he did not want kids.

5. I did not think I had any doubts. It's easy to look back and realize I sensed that he did not have the motivation to start his own business and to begin to make some decent money. I figured he would get moving when we married and especially if we had children, but I found out later I was wrong on both counts. He did not want children and had no ambition.

6. It turns out Tad is a narcissist and a gambler. He never talked about his gambling before we married, and I had no idea how much of his meager salary he lost each week.

7. I still believe he was attracted to me in the beginning, but there's nothing more between us now. Tad used to have a good build, but he has gained about 30 pounds since our wedding, including a large gut, but refuses to consider how this interferes with our sex life. Not only is he less attractive to me, but his stomach actually gets in the way. The funny part is, he acts as if he's less interested in me, maybe looking for other women, and I do not even care.
8. Realistically, I have not changed one bit physically. Still weigh what I did on our wedding day, still fit in the same clothes I did then. Go to the gym four times a week and keep in excellent physical health and condition. I am probably more depressed than I have ever felt. My marriage is a complete loss, and he is a dud to have around, with no interest in improving himself or our relationship.
9. Boy, this could be a dissertation. I wish he had shown some motivation in some area, his work, his physical condition, us, anything. He let himself go physically and gained all that weight, but if he at least demonstrated some responsibility for my feelings, maybe we could have worked on things. But he showed no love, affection, attention, or any acknowledgment of my worth as a wife.
10. What I wish I did differently was make my discontent clearer much earlier, or maybe even divorced within the first two years, instead of thinking it would get better. I should have said "goodbye" much sooner, instead of being a glutton for punishment.
11. Next time I am going to look for a deeper emotional attachment and find someone interested in improving himself, his career, and our relationship. I think I misinterpreted sex as love in those early days. That is a mistake I will not make again.

Cornelia is a thoughtful woman and reported that the questionnaire helped her realize she was living the life her family thought was right for her, rather than what she needed for herself. She became aware of how little importance she placed on her husband's lack of introspective ability or his lack of motivation to improve himself. Cornelia had been divorced for two years, was dating, and felt that she had the tools she needed to avoid the same mistakes.

2.6 A successful marriage requires adjustments, and maybe you two did not make them

Life is very often about compromises, and marriages even more so. No situation is perfect. Even the deepest love requires attention and nurturing and effort. No relationship will succeed if you take it—or each other—for granted.

We reap what we sow.

Philip is a handsome man. Successful in business. Well educated. His wife, Samantha, is nothing less than gorgeous. And bright. And funny. Philip and Samantha were about as much fun as any couple you may have the good fortune to meet. They were welcome at every social event, and it is not too much to say they added a touch of glamour when they appeared. After a few years, they were thrilled at the birth of each of their two daughters, and instantly became loving and devoted parents. They were a golden couple.

And then the pilot light went out.

As much as Philip loved his daughters, he began to grow weary of the domestic life they were obliged to lead. No more late nights partying in New York City. No more spur of the moment trips to Vermont or Florida or the Caribbean. In his view, at least, there was no more romance. He started spending more time at the office, and when he went on the road he went for business. Alone.

As for Samantha, her reaction was predictable. She felt rejected and unappreciated, both of which were true. She felt that she had been left to do the lion's share of the parenting. And then she retaliated in age-old fashion—she lost interest in sex.

The story of how their marriage imploded is a cautionary tale. Neither of them was good at verbalizing their issues, concerns, and complaints. Philip and Samantha had built their rapport on passion and pleasure. They lacked the skills to deal with any sort of trouble, even when they saw a therapist.

And then Philip met Shantal.

She was not much younger than Samantha and certainly not as beautiful. But she restored what was now missing in Philip's life. Excitement. Ardor. Sex.

He was totally selfish, ignoring the increasing tension in his household as he spent more evenings out, coming home late, sleeping in the guest bedroom more and more frequently. His life had become a cliché, but he did not stop to consider the consequences—as already stated, that was not his long suit—and he failed to recognize that such things never have a happy ending.

Shantal had her own agenda. Like most third parties in these triangles, she did not concern herself with the fact that her lover was a married man cheating on his wife, which should have told her something about his character. She wanted him for herself and, as time went on, she decided to take matters into her own hands. One night, after too many glasses of chardonnay, she called Samantha and told her everything.

The end game was predictable. Philip and Samantha went through a bitter divorce and, despite the fact that they would share two daughters for the rest of their lives, they have never been able to create a workable means of communicating. She would never forgive him and in an ironic exhibition of egotism, he resented her anger. Shantal, of course, was abandoned in the process. She had been nothing more than a distraction, a bit player in their drama, but that was something she only realized when it was too late.

Both Philip and Samantha ultimately found new partners, both married and both were again divorced. Why? Because even when their marriage was over, neither was willing to explore the reasons their wonderful connection had failed. Neither had made any concessions to the other. Neither dealt with the obligations they had to each other or their children, not once the music stopped. Neither took any responsibility for what went wrong. And so, as they say, the past became prologue, and each continues to struggle into the future.

Do not let this happen to you as you traverse the hazards of splitting.

2.7 Divorce and Religion.

Some of our clients presented religion, spirituality, or a specific belief in a deity as being instrumental in their divorce decision-making process and post-divorce coping. While we recognize that faith is not important to everyone who is considering a divorce, it is worth examining for everyone. You never know who you will meet next, and what may or may not be important. Based on the intensity of feeling from those who raised the issue, these concepts are an important part of who they are, so it is valuable to have some insight into that.

In our work, we have seen both men and women wrestle with the thought that their religion demanded they stay married for spiritual reasons, when everything else about their life was screaming for them to run. If your religious beliefs have you feeling that the demise of your marriage has caused you to fail in those commitments, then we urge you to speak with someone who is trained to counsel in your particular faith, such as a priest, minister, rabbi or imam.

Divorce is never easy, and if your religious belief plays a role in how you see it, the process becomes even harder. Neither of us is trained clergy and it is not our role to advise you with respect to your religious beliefs, but whatever your religion, we believe the God you worship would want you to be safe and happy. We doubt that God would want you to stay in a situation where you are being deceived, abused, mistreated, or otherwise made miserable.

The theme presented by most people who discuss this area focuses on the sadness and guilt they experience, whether they have initiated the divorce or are the spouse being left behind. It will become a primary task for you to find forgiveness in your faith, for both you and your spouse, regardless of whatever cruel treatment your spouse has engaged in. However, that forgiveness does not imply a reversal of the divorce decision or that you should be able to live with that person. Sadness and guilt do not mean you want to reverse the divorce decision.

Sadness and guilt are part of divorce. If you are religious, talking openly with God, through prayer, can also lead to a feeling of God's forgiveness.

<u>Religion should not be an impediment to happiness.</u>

Jerry was a highly emotional and sensitive person who was about to file for a divorce after seven years of marriage to Jill, who became involved with another man. He was convinced he wanted the divorce but had to address the dilemma his religious beliefs presented. His faith frowned on divorce, but he also believed that God wanted him to be happy. Knowing that Jill was sleeping with someone else made the thought of staying with her excruciatingly painful, but his religion told him his vows were an unbreakable bond.

Complicating matters was the fact that Jerry was the leader of his church's weekly Bible discussion group. He sang in the choir on Sundays, and most of his friends were members of the different church groups of which he was a member. That left him betraying the tenets of his faith, and fearing the disapproving judgments of his friends and fellow parishioners. Being kind and sensitive, he did not want to reveal Jill's infidelity, but without that, how would these people understand what he was going through? She was also a member of the church, and despite her betrayal he could not bring himself to damn her in that way.

Throughout his life, when faced with a difficult decision, he would pray a great deal about it, asking for direction. For a period of time, after learning that his wife was being unfaithful, Jerry prayed that his marriage would be saved, that Jill would give up this other man and return her love to him. But when that prayer was not answered for several years, he wondered if that was some sort of divine intervention, a sign that God was encouraging the divorce.

But he could not be sure.

In the end, the key to Jerry's release from the grip of this impasse was a true awareness of what he really owed himself and his God. Through counselling and discussions with his priest, he began to understand. He was respecting his marriage by not disgracing his unfaithful wife.

Would God not appreciate that? He was escaping a loveless, hopeless marriage. Would God not want him to be released from that misery? He was honoring God by his continuing commitment to his faith. Would God not love him for that? He could not sacrifice his own happiness for the views of others. Would his true friends not rally to support him?

Jerry's priest encouraged him to share his divorce decision with members of the church groups to which he belonged—and from whom he feared criticism and rejection. He was surprised when three men in the Bible study group shared their own stories. They were divorced and remarried and were understanding of his decision. He also heard from several women in the group who supported the belief that God's plan for any of us is to find true love, the commitment of our loved one, and to be happy in our marriage. They also all supported the belief that one cannot have a successful marriage unless both accept that their vows were holy in the eyes of God and not to be betrayed. He obviously welcomed this view, even though he did not reveal Jill's behavior.

Clients who have faced these issues have ultimately found that their friends did not abandon them. Continuing their church attendance and, as in Jerry's case, participation in the various religious activities he had been involved in, helped to strengthen them and become more comfortable that—in the eyes of God—their divorce was accepted, and was both morally and spiritually the correct decision

2.8 The purpose of all this is to help you understand why you are going where you are going

You are embarking on one of the most difficult and perilous expeditions of your life—we hope you did not skimp on the tasks we laid out in this chapter to help you figure out how you got to this point of departure.

We realize we had you do a deep dive into these issues, but if you were thinking about going on safari in Africa or an exploration of the Amazon, it is highly unlikely you would just pack an overnight bag and jump on the next flight. You would think it through, carefully chart your course and make all the required preparations—but before any of that, you would know why you are going.

DOWNLOAD #2 To help free yourself from the repetitive thoughts about why your marriage failed, we encourage you to listen to the program at: www.theroadtosplitsville.com and go to the link for Splitsville Download #2

Chapter 3
How To Deal With The Potholes You Will Encounter Along The Journey

"My mission in life is not merely to survive, but to thrive; and to do so with some passion, some compassion, some humor, and some style."
—Maya Angelou

In the brief first chapter, we explained what this book is about. In the second, we helped you examine why you have embarked on this very difficult path—and you have done some heavy lifting, having a look at what went wrong and how you found yourself on the road to Splitsville. Now, as we forge ahead on our journey, we want to assist you in bracing for the inevitable upset you will face along the way and prepare you to build a happier future.

As we acknowledge throughout this book, and regardless of the factors that led you to this moment, your divorce will undoubtedly create emotional issues you will need to handle. When the battle is done and the smoke finally clears, even if you feel your spouse is the one responsible for the failure of your marriage, there will remain some level of distress to be faced.

Let's say you were loyal and loving and supportive during your marriage, while your spouse was cheating on you with impunity, and you know you are well rid of them. You will still need to deal with the hurt that comes from that sort of betrayal, right? Or flip it around. Say you're the abuser, the alcoholic, the liar—pick a negative quality that suits you—and now you've lost someone who loved you in ways you fear no one else may ever feel about you again. That's a difficult prospect to face.

Then there is the most common situation of all—you both blew it. Your spouse became a constant critic, and you reacted with anger, perhaps even violence. Or you both cheated. Or you were a lousy parent and your spouse responded by becoming so devoted to the children that you were ignored in the process, maybe withholding sex or simply depriving you of affection. Or, as the marriage went along, neither of you properly supported or understood the other.

The examples go on and on, but hopefully, you wrote these things down in the course of our questionnaires in Chapter 2. Now that you are done summarizing what you each did to destroy what began as a union of love and promise, it is time to move forward without carrying the pain from those mistakes. Even more important, we want to help you avoid repeating your share of those blunders in the future.

Our first bit of advice on this subject may be surprising, but it concerns the natural desire to share details of your failed marriage with others. Before you do, take a moment to consider the people you have known who were eager to recount their own divorce tales. Think about how they believed their story was unique and fascinating and something others want to hear. Now, get this loud and clear—THEY WERE WRONG!

We are not denying the importance of confiding your hurt to a close friend or two or seeking the guidance of a professional counselor. All of that is critical to the healing process.

What does not help, however, is inserting yourself into a group of acquaintances at a cocktail party and regaling them with every gory detail of your ordeal, sharing all the things you despise about your spouse, how great—or awful—your lawyer was, and otherwise sucking all of the oxygen from the room. Not only is this not useful to you, but your friends will inevitably begin avoiding you like a leper. Whether you like it or not, there is a limit to the compassion of others, and rather than empathizing with your plight they will likely end up seeing you as a crashing bore. Remember, they have their own problems, and suffering through your whining description of a failed marriage will do nothing to endear you to them.

As we say, save that for one or two of your closest friends and, if you feel it will be helpful, your therapist.

Our second recommendation is to use the energy you might waste telling your story to everyone you meet by having a serious look at what you are feeling now. As we emphasized in Chapter 2, you need to understand what brought you to today. As we also stressed earlier, this includes going all the way back to the genesis of your marriage, a review of how it all began and then honestly appraising how things went bad.

3.1 The emotional factors you will need to face.

What follows is not intended as an exhaustive discussion of all the elements possible in failed marriages. It is designed to help you achieve a level of self-awareness so you can get past the things that are eating at you. Along the way, you can fill in the blanks for yourself as you see fit.

Although marriages break up for many different reasons, we will begin with an example that is one of the most common and difficult to overcome—the discovery that your partner has been cheating. You may question why we have chosen to use the word "cheating" instead of the more commonly used term "infidelity," or the expression "being unfaithful." The reason is simple—most of our patients and clients who discover their spouse has become sexually involved with another person feel just that, CHEATED. They believed their marriage was a sacred pact, one of the most important terms of which was the promise not to go outside the marriage for sex, romance, or intimacy. And yet, according to a publication of the Institute for Family Studies,* over forty percent of married couples are faced with the discovery that one or both partners have betrayed that agreement.

Let us compare this to some other situations. Say you are engaged in business with a partner and find they are embezzling money. You feel

CHEATED, right? If you buy a used car from a dealer who tells you the vehicle was never in an accident and then discover it had been repaired after a serious wreck, you feel CHEATED, correct? If you are playing cards with friends, and you find that one of them is sneaking a peek at your hand, you feel CHEATED, do you not?

The sense of betrayal you feel when your spouse has cheated on you is obviously far, far more intense than any of those mundane examples, with a resultant array of emotional problems and pain.

There are a number of reasons why a spouse might cheat. In some cases, the individual has come into the marriage carrying baggage that interferes with their ability to maintain a committed relationship. But that does not excuse the betrayal.

There are other situations, when the cheating spouse no longer wants to be married, and it is really an exit strategy. But their behavior is still wrong. Very often, when this occurs, there is typically no willingness by the cheating party to discuss the causes or to try to work things out.

Even worse, there may be no signs of remorse.

If your marriage has been destroyed by cheating, give yourself permission to experience the normal feelings of shame, anger, hurt, disappointment, guilt, embarrassment, failure, and the tendency to indulge in self-blame. Going through all or any of these feelings is normal and inherent in the act of being cheated upon. There has been damage which often leaves you with a fear you will never again be able to trust.

But you will. You will come to realize that some marriages are not meant to be saved. The anguish you feel will diminish over time, and that will happen more quickly if you accept that your spouse was flawed in ways you could not do anything about.

Another common category of problems is grouped together by leading researchers as *contempt.** Some experts believe it is the number one predictor of divorce, defining contempt as acts of disrespect, repeated instances of mocking the spouse, or the use of sarcasm and condescension.

No matter what form such contempt takes—name-calling, ridicule, or body language that communicates disdain—it is poisonous to a relationship as their judgmental attitude demonstrates a toxic sense of superiority. One researcher summarizes the contempt as if your partner is saying, "I'm better than you, and you are lesser than I."* As you think back on instances of contempt in your own marriage, you will see how those attacks on your self-worth increased the likelihood of further conflict. It is all but impossible to resolve marital discord when your spouse is insulting you or asserting superiority.

If you have experienced contempt from your partner, you will surely recognize the unhappy environment it creates. Whatever else is troubling you, contempt will just keep making things worse. It becomes all but impossible to engage in positive discussions about the relationship when there is such difficulty getting beyond the argument mode.

Sound familiar?

The important thing to remember is that contempt is generally a symptom and, if you go back and review your answers to the Spousal Attachment Survey, you should see the threads of discord that led to those unpleasant and painful exchanges.

3.2 Some stages you may pass through along this journey.

Let us begin with a case history:

Frances

Frances sat there crying,

"I think I'm going crazy, I swing back and forth between a sense of relief, a buoyant feeling and then suddenly a sense of deep sadness, almost depression and fear. I can't breathe normally. You know, I try, but I can't catch my breath. I sit there sure I will die. I even get chest pains and become sure I will have a heart attack. I think I'm going crazy. Do you think I need medicine? I don't know what's happening, I can't seem to keep it together.

I'm not eating enough, can't sleep, don't even want to get dressed in the morning. I even stopped brushing my teeth."

After going on about this sense of desperation, she shared another dominant emotion-- anger. She becomes so angry at her husband she can hardly see straight. The rage was evident as she explained that she discovered, "He's been screwing someone else, and has been for at least two years." Through a cascade of tears, she said, "I wanted to kill both of them. It's some slut in his office, I know who she is, but he's such a liar he denies it right to my face, then refuses to go with me for counseling." She managed a deep, uneven breath. "I thought I did everything to make him happy. I don't know, maybe I didn't. He wanted me to do some things in bed, you know, things I thought were disgusting."

Frances stood up and began waving her fist in the air. "We exchanged vows in front of God and our family. How could he just disregard that? I go to church, always ask him to come with me, but he never does. We met in church, he used to go all the time. Do I deserve this?" She sat again, looking totally deflated. "We're married six years, how could he do this to me? I'm so upset, I find I'm drinking too much. Am I going to end up with a drinking problem on top of everything else? Do I need to be medicated? All I know, is that he's a cheater and I want no part of him. It's over, and I just want to make him pay. I intend to take him for all he's worth."

Frances was furious, confused, and her thoughts flew from one thing to another, questioning her own sanity as she dealt with anger, panic, and anxiety.

At that point, she needed to take stock of all she was going through. The sense of betrayal and the emotional pain. She had made the biggest and most significant decision of her life, which left her to wrestle with critical aspects of her self-image, not to mention the practical ramifications of divorce. She was a sensitive woman and there is no reason she would go through this without feeling uncertainty and fears about the future.

It is normal to feel any or all of these things. Even doubts about your decision to end the marriage will sometimes take hold. The most useful reaction is to figure out what happened in full detail. This is why we asked you to answer these questionnaires and work toward an understanding that will eventually help the pain go away. Emotional swings between hope and despair come with the territory.

There may have been times when you felt this way yourself. It is important to know that it is normal to experience these feelings during the divorce process. The feeling of "going crazy" is not unusual and entirely normal. This flood of sensations may have you swinging between despair over your marriage ending to the fear that your future will be no better.

It is also common for you to keep re-living what happened. You may hope to identify all the sources of your pain in an attempt to get it to dissipate, but do not get on that merry-go-round. It is useless and harmful to constantly think of how things could have gone differently, or how you are to blame for your spouse's betrayals. It is far more productive to accept that you played some part—large or small—in your marriage ending on the rocks. It is better to realize that all of the repair efforts you have tried—such as convincing your spouse to attend counseling, employing different communication techniques, or even offering a restart of your relationship—have all failed. Face reality. The fault is not yours alone, nor does it belong solely to your spouse.

As already discussed, there are a number of factors that make a relationship either work or cause it to implode. Although it may be difficult to accept, our core personalities do not change much, if at all, once we reach adulthood. We are who we are. and your marriage became what it was destined to be.

You may ask yourself why you didn't leave sooner, or behave differently, or take some action you now regret not taking—but the result would have been the same. You are far better off using that energy to forgive yourself and preparing for the next phase of your life.

You will feel upset regardless of how well you approach things. This is predictable after the commitment you made at the outset of your marriage, and the current realization that it is over. Grief is part of the program, and it carries with it other deep emotions as it runs its course. There may be denial and depression, or an attempt to minimize the importance of the loss. Anger will flare up with a desire for some sort of revenge against your spouse:

"I'll take him to the cleaners."

"I'll find a woman twenty years younger than she is and show her off all over town."

"I'll never let him speak to our children again."

"I'll make sure she never gets to spend a dime of my money."

Give yourself time to process and digest these natural reactions. As time passes, the wounds will heal. Eventually, you will come to view the loss as an event that happened in the past, something that is no longer a part of your day-to-day life. It may not feel like that to you now, but the human mind has an amazing capacity to dismiss the pain. If that were not true, what woman would ever put herself through childbirth more than once?

When your grieving begins to subside, you will begin to mobilize and get on with your life. We say, THE SOONER THE BETTER! Even if you find the sadness and grief persisting as you move on, that's okay. Focus on spending more of your energy for the future and less for the past.

We are not pretending that divorce is easy. You will experience a host of unpleasant feelings along the way, but how you handle them will define what the future holds in store. That includes the way you approach the divorce itself. The central relationship of your existence is ending, which means many daily routines will no longer be part of your life. You will also be involved in a legal process, perhaps for the first time, and you have to steer your way along that path while you are in the grip of those volatile emotions.

We are here to help you with all of that.

An interesting phenomenon is that, no matter how bad your marriage may have been, you may still love your spouse. For some time, the two of you were attached, and your spouse was a part of your existence. You shared a home and maybe a family. Although you rate your relationship as a failure, it is rare for everything to have been wrong. At some point, there was a powerful force between the two of you and it's natural that you would go through a period feeling a sense of disbelief that this is happening to you.

We want to help you understand and accept, that no matter how certain you are that you have finally made the right decision to free yourself from an unhappy marriage, it will still be a tough journey. Many experts report that people going through a divorce experience emotional stages that are similar to grieving the death of a loved one. Although these vary, one such list is:

Denial

Shock

Pain and guilt

Anger

Depression

The upward turn

Reconstruction and working through

Acceptance and hope

There is a large part of you committed to your decision, but you may still have to go through some or all, of these transitions. This is called *life*. You are not an automaton, and we want you to be prepared and not to feel alone or abnormal as you hit bumps in the road. Let's have a look at some of these key phases.

DENIAL

Denial is a normal emotion during the early stages of divorce, a natural reluctance within you that refuses to accept that the relationship is over. As you wrestle with all of the ambivalent feelings related to the breakup of your marriage, even as you convince yourself that you are one hundred percent sure, there will still be a part of you that finds it hard to believe this is happening.

Rather than resist it, you should recognize that denial is a powerful coping tool and, in many ways, will help you confront the reality of the situation. As you go over and over in your mind whether this is the right thing to do, denial will permit you to see the "other side" of the argument until you finally reach the point of total conviction you are right. Give yourself a pat on the shoulder after you have gone through denial, it is a healthy psychological stage to take yourself through.

GUILT

Guilt is one of the most wasteful and destructive emotions we face. When going through a divorce, some people convince themselves their behavior is responsible for the failure. They often imagine things they should or should not have done. But what is the point of all that? You have done what you have done, why relive it? To punish yourself? To wallow in regret?

In most divorces, this "self-blame game" is way out of proportion to what truly transpired. Take time to reflect on the true reasons you are feeling guilty. Guilt can be minimized by realizing that the issues gnawing at you are really minor parts of what happened to your marriage. Focus on the future and the things within your control. Consider that any guilt you may feel is unfounded and is produced only because you are being too hard on yourself.

You certainly have made mistakes, maybe you even believe the collapse of the relationship is all your fault—no matter how large a role you played, you can be assured it is not all your doing. Take it easy on yourself. Guilt is like a 100-pound weight strapped to your back. You have to get rid of it before you can walk upright and move forward.

SHOCK

Once you have traveled through the denial stage, depending on where you are in the divorce progression, you may face pure shock. By shock, we mean that sense of panic that comes when you ask yourself questions like:

"What did I do?"

"What will I do next?"

"How am I going to survive this?"

This sort of fear is natural. After all, you've invested much of your life in the marriage. You may be afraid of facing life alone. There will be financial worries, physical concerns, and the prospect of abject loneliness.

We know, as we spell out those ideas, they are not exactly going to cheer you up, but we are also here to tell you that it will work out. One of the reasons we are speaking to you is to provide that assurance—you got yourself into this marriage, it did not work out as you had hoped and planned, and so you are getting out. A new life will then stretch out before you, like a beautiful, unexplored road. Once you have completed the journey to Splitsville, the opportunities for freedom, happiness and new love are on the other side waiting for you. It's natural to have doubts about that now, and it may be difficult to envision the sunshine beyond the current storm clouds, but your feelings are temporary and will gradually give way to the actions necessary to make a new life.

ANGER

Anger is another completely normal part of this sequence of emotions, sort of the flip side of guilt. It is an expected and healthy reaction to your partner's actions, especially if you see your spouse as responsible for the failure of your marriage. Without feelings of anger, you would not be able to take a stand against the injustices you have suffered. Anger should be viewed as an internal alarm, telling you that things were not right, not fair, not deserved. Once you move through denial, guilt, and shock, it will be natural to begin thinking, "How could I have been treated this way?" You are likely to use choice words to describe your spouse you may not customarily use in public. That is all fine, provided you do not allow yourself to *become* your anger.

Allow yourself the privilege of thinking how unfairly you were treated, allocate the blame for the collapse of the relationship, and permit yourself the anger you feel over your spouse's behavior. Our advice for this stage is, "Have at it."

But limit those with whom you share those disparaging and insulting remarks about your spouse. Instead of ranting to everyone you know, focus on your internal conversations. Then, our next instruction is, "Do your best to let it go." Anger, like guilt, is corrosive. Your marriage has failed because your spouse is a [*fill in the blank*]. That is enough to suffer. Do not allow ongoing anger to cause you additional upset.

DEPRESSION

This is a tough one, because depression can be a debilitating emotion. Denial, shock, guilt, and anger all involve some sort of internal or external action. Depression leaves you feeling weak, deprives you of energy and is generally a state of unhappy malaise. We wish there were an easy fix for this, but on this one you need to work with us!

Ending a marriage is difficult, as we have repeatedly acknowledged. Even though you have decided that your relationship was at a dead end and that it was self-destructive for you to continue, a sense of loss and sadness is inevitable as you watch your hopes and dreams for that partnership evaporate.

It is critical that we point out the difference between sadness and the too often used and confused term of depression. Many people going through a divorce describe themselves as depressed and far too often get feedback, especially from those who are trying to be helpful, agreeing that they are depressed. Unfortunately, those well-meaning friends do not understand what depression means. The term *depression* should only be used to describe a mood disorder that causes a persistent feeling of despair and withdrawal from everything pleasurable.

Do not travel down that rabbit hole.

Feeling down or sad or having some of the same behaviors and symptoms of true depression does not mean you are suffering from clinical depression. However, there is such a thing as *situational depression*, which is temporary and can be triggered by your feelings. As an example, if you are afraid of tigers and you are walking through the woods in Connecticut there is no reality to the possibility you will encounter a tiger, and therefore no real trigger. On the other hand, if you are walking through those woods in Connecticut and have a fear of snakes, this has a possible reality base to it and may cause realistic anxiety. The same formula applies to depression. A divorce is a real loss with a justifiable reason to feel despair, loss, and the sense you are immobilized. This is situational depression and very different from clinical depression. You are probably sad rather than depressed, although at times, they may seem to be the same feeling.

Most people going through a divorce experience some degree of situational depression as part of the normal grieving process over the loss it represents.

The grieving process is natural and unique to each individual and shares some of the same features of depression. Both grief and depression may involve intense sorrow and withdrawal from usual activities, but they are different in important ways.

It would be a disservice to minimize or dismiss the possible emotional reactions you are having. For instance, you may find yourself crying when you think about the decision and what lies ahead. Give yourself the permission to go through that heartache. When you're going through the emotional wringer and dealing with major life changes, you need to take care of yourself and work through those feelings. Give yourself permission to feel any emotion that besets you. Allow yourself the inescapable mood swings, from being hopeful to feeling despair. You may have panic attacks and feel uncontrollable rage at one moment, then a sense of freedom and optimism the next.

It is all part of the journey.

ACCEPTANCE

The final stage we hope for you is acceptance, which does not suggest that you are suddenly going to be overwhelmed by happiness or miraculously free from all the grief and pain of the divorce. It simply means that you have finally realized what the divorce represents, that you have acknowledged that this is your future and that it is real. This is the stage where you realize that you need to get deeper into yourself, where you truly understand what has happened and when you see a path for moving past it. This is when you experience relief and a willingness to begin considering your future. You may get there on your own, you may want some professional help, or you may have a close friend who assists you in reaching this rite of passage.

We hope that one of the benefits of reading this book is the realization that you are not alone in what you are experiencing, either during and after the divorce. It should also help you see that you are not unusual in the things you are going through, which are part of a normal process for most people in a divorce.

No one expects you to immediately feel better because you have accepted the divorce, but entering the acceptance stage means that you are moving in the right direction. There is sunlight at the end of the road, even if you are not yet there. Give yourself time and permission to begin thinking about your future. Make plans, find things to do, places to go, and people you look forward to seeing. We are not talking about a miraculous shedding of pain, but rather, allowing yourself the vision of freedom and joy that lies ahead. This is a time to appreciate yourself. You have traveled through a difficult series of phases, while learning and benefitting from them. Join the millions of other people who have been through this momentous event and have survived in so many excellent ways.

It is time to build a new life.

3.3 Finding the tools to help you get over whatever is eating you

As we have tried to point out in this chapter, getting over whatever troubles you during and after the divorce is critical in getting on with your life and coping with the many feelings that will periodically overwhelm you. Here are some practical tools that will help you get through that process:

1. Carefully choose with whom you associate during this process. Recognize those who are sensitive to your situation and those who are not. Surround yourself with people who bring a positive attitude. You may find the need to limit existing friendships, at least for a while, and to avoid spending time with those who prevent you from getting over your divorce. The simplest way to determine who is good for you and who is not is to be aware of how you feel about yourself when they are around.

2. There may be times when you feel you need to let loose and basically just vent. That desire or drive is understandable, but be aware that constantly talking and thinking about the divorce will create a negative attitude and impair positive thinking. Being tuned into what you are permitting to go on in your head is an important avenue to getting over whatever is eating you. As the song says, "accentuate the positive, eliminate the negative."

3. It is normal, during and after a divorce, to overthink what might have been or should have been done. Our advice is to do everything possible to abandon those "woulda, coulda, shoulda" thoughts. If you are this far along the road to Splitsville, it is destructive to spend your time wondering whether the marriage could have been saved if you had done certain things differently. This is not the same as examining why the marriage failed so you can do better in the future. Simply dwelling on past mistakes is not productive. You cannot negotiate this trip forward with your focus on the rear-view mirror. The decision to divorce has been made, and you need to keep your eyes and thoughts on the road ahead.

4. As we have repeatedly acknowledged, emotional turmoil is part of this journey— it is normal to feel anger, confusion, fear, sadness, and other disturbing emotions. If you are having trouble dealing with these waves of upset, we never want you to bury those emotions, and it may be worthwhile for you to seek professional assistance. Divorce counseling can be just as valuable as marriage counseling, so do not hesitate to find a good therapist to help you work things through.

5. One way some people attempt to deal with their distress is to use alcohol or narcotics to dull the pain. It should be obvious, but we feel compelled to say it anyway—be careful! Not only can these substances be physically dangerous, but their use does nothing to heal you or solve your problems. Relying on substances to cope with whatever is eating you will only extend the grieving process, create a new issue, and interfere with constructing a new life.

6. You may find that frequent thoughts about your ex will pop up. This is understandable. After all, you had a daily relationship and interaction with your ex, even if it was a negative one. Give yourself a break and realize that letting go of that connection will take some time to resolve. In fact, acknowledge yourself for being a caring person, then let it go.

7. Instead of reliving the mistakes of your marriage or wondering what your ex is doing, spend that time and energy recalling who you were before the marriage. Get into who you believed you were before you married. Allow yourself to create a "bucket list" of all the things you wanted to try that you did not—all those things you may be able to do now! To help get over whatever is eating you about the divorce, take the opportunity to imagine the life you want for yourself. Think of things like a writing workshop, travel, music lessons, an art class, a culinary program, getting your pilot's license, and so forth. Then, do not hesitate. As soon as possible, start making these things real. Get back to being YOU!
8. As a corollary to rediscovering yourself, enjoy being single. We are not minimizing the pain of your loss, but to help you get over the lingering parts of the divorce, begin looking at the positive aspects of being single. Instead of seeing yourself alone, see yourself as FREE! You are no longer accountable for eating and sleeping schedules that are imposed upon you, nor do you have to answer for your partner's needs. Stay up late if you like, spend your time and money any way you want, do what gives you pleasure. Never forget—this is why you are making this journey. Enjoy the ride!

Jim

Jim is gay. He explained that he and his husband, Philip, were having a difficult time with their impending divorce. It was raising a lot of painful memories and feelings for both of them. They had been partners for eight years, having married as soon as the law permitted.

Jim said, "We shared the same type of love vows any heterosexual couple would make. We went through the ring exchange ritual. Neither of us wanted this to be regarded as a gay marriage, but rather as a marriage just as it would be for any other couple. We were living in Arizona, but my company transferred me to New York City and we settled in a town in Connecticut where we sensed we would be accepted. From the time we first moved in, the people we befriended did not regard us as just partners, companions or friends living together, but as a real married couple. It was comfortable and gratifying."

Then he described the pain. The people around them, even their best friends, began acting in a totally different manner when they told them they were divorcing. Jim felt as if they were not experiencing the same issues and emotional turmoil as a heterosexual couple in the midst of a divorce.

He said, "Their reaction is as if we are simply breaking up, as if it's not a painful thing for us because suddenly they do not see us as partners in a traditional marriage. I want some sort of acknowledgment that our emotions are the same as they would be for any heterosexual couple. We are sad, angry at each other, fearful for what the future might bring, often feeling so anxious that we can't concentrate, and depressed. I know these are the same feelings that all couples go through, but it feels more intense since our friends are not taking our marriage seriously. Some of them are even saying that the usual divorce laws that apply to heterosexual couples do not apply to same-sex couples, which is not true!"

When Jim began to discuss the things that precipitated the divorce decision, he could have been describing the breakdown of any heterosexual marriage. Jim explained that, although it took him five months of secretive investigation, he was finally able to support his suspicions that Philip was having an affair. He found that Philip had been involved in an intimate relationship with a colleague at work and, when Jim confronted him, he admitted he had fallen in love with this other man. His reasons for what he described as "falling out of love with Jim" were vague, but he certainly was not taking the blame.

Jim said, "This is something that I really struggle with. I am constantly trying to figure out how I am to blame. The arguments, the constant bickering, the growing distance between us, now made sense."

Jim went over the emotional turmoil he was suffering through, and it was the same sort of issue as any couple going through a divorce would face. Jim explained that, even though they were well on their way to getting the divorce, the pain for each of them was considerable. They are having difficulty living with each other while the process takes place, and feeling an intense resentment toward each other.

Jim began a course of counseling, the treatment being the same as it would have proceeded with a heterosexual couple. Unfortunately, Jim's upset was worsened by how he was treated by those he regarded as friends. As it turned out, they did not really respect the sanctity of his marriage. Empathy, understanding and support are things anyone on the journey to Splitsville can use.

3.4 A few brief remarks about your physical health

Throughout this book, we endeavor to help you negotiate the emotional and practical aspects of your journey. Along the way, we reference certain issues that relate to your physical health, but we wanted to make a few basic points here.

Many people cope with the pressures and upset of divorce through a variety of harmful activities. These may include alcohol abuse, narcotics, over-eating and so forth. Even if you avoid these pitfalls, you may suffer anxiety, a lack of proper sleep, failure to exercise, or other syndromes that can negatively affect your well-being.

We realize it is difficult to sidestep all of those problems all the time, but we ask you to always remember to HONOR YOURSELF. That's right, self-love is important on so many levels, and by that we do not mean narcissism or selfishness. We merely want you to understand that you should always take care of your body—it is not only what the world sees first of you, it is also what encompasses your brain, soul, and spirit. You cannot be effective in addressing the issues of divorce—or the enjoyment of life, for that matter—unless you are in proper and healthy shape. If you allow yourself, or even worse *cause* yourself, to become overweight, out-of-shape or ill, how will you be able to handle everything else?

Watch your diet. Engage in a serious workout routine. As obvious as this may sound, create the best you possible so you will be in an optimum position to enjoy your new and exciting future!

DOWNLOAD #3 *In order to help you relax and better deal with these feelings we have included download #3 for you to listen to. Use this download to cope better with the natural course of divorce experiences. Visit www.theroadtosplitsville.com and go to the link for Splitsville Download #3*

CHAPTER 4
CHOOSING THE VEHICLE TO GET YOU TO SPLITSVILLE

You have now engaged in an honest, soul-searching appraisal of your personal circumstances, and we hope you are crystal clear about why you have made the decision to divorce. You have also done work to understand and address the various emotions you will encounter on this expedition, and we believe that will help to ease the path forward.

It is now time to embark on the journey.

This chapter is intended to provide the road map to get you to Splitsville. There is no telling how smooth or bumpy the road ahead will be—some of that will depend on your attitude toward the process, some will depend on your spouse's attitude, and part of it will be the result of influences that are beyond your control. But no trip can begin until you decide how you are going to get to your destination, right? Are you going to take a car, train, bus, or plane? Are you going to walk, hitchhike, or have a friend take you?

The same is true here. There are a number of viable options, each of which should be considered before taking the first step. It would be helpful if you and your spouse could discuss these together, but that will depend on the level of acrimony in your breakup. Keep in mind, most states provide for the right to divorce on some sort of "no fault" basis. In the old days you needed a private eye with a camera to catch your spouse with their lover in flagrante delicto at some seedy motel; or have evidence of abuse; or prove abandonment; or otherwise establish a legal basis for ending the marriage. Now you can get a divorce by essentially telling the court you want one.

This means that the bad deeds of the parties will generally be ignored by the judge, who will view your split as if it were the liquidation of a small business. The tawdry details of the breakup will generally have no relevance. People are astounded by this, but it is true. No matter how rotten you believe your spouse was, it will have almost no impact on the financial results.

What, then, are various ways to reach your destination? We will lay those out, but first you need to understand the factors that will be considered in this process. As you may know, the mechanics of obtaining the actual judgment of divorce are relatively easy once you resolve the tough issues—splitting assets and debts; deciding who will keep the place where the two of you currently live (the "marital home"); future spousal support (called "alimony" in some jurisdictions); and all the matters involving children, including support, custody, visitation, health care, and education.

To begin with, you or your spouse (or one of your attorneys) will file an Action for Divorce in the court where one or both of you live. You will go through some "discovery" processes which will be described in more detail below, but which generally involve the exchange of Financial Statements, bank and credit card documents, and so forth. If things become complicated there may be depositions—these are sessions in the office of one of the lawyers where you and your spouse each give testimony in response to questions posed by the attorney for the other side, which is recorded by a stenographer.

Whatever decisions you make as you move along this path, the more complicated and contentious things become, the more costly things will be. Regardless of your financial circumstances, since everything is relative, divorce can become ridiculously expensive if you and/or your spouse are not sensible. We submit to you here a critical piece of information, which is true in almost every case, with rare exceptions:

WITHIN A REASONABLE MARGIN FOR ERROR, THE ULTIMATE FINANCIAL RESULT OF YOUR DIVORCE WAS PREDICTABLE THE DAY YOU DECIDED TO SPLIT!

That is the truth. Your assets, debts, income, and expenses are what they are. Once you impart that information to any good matrimonial attorney, they will be able to tell you where your case is going to end up, allowing for a small margin for error. Do you and your spouse really want to spend a lot of money paying lawyers who already know that the final terms will not change? Would you not rather put that money into your children's college account? Or for you to buy a new car? Or to pay off debts? Or to take a vacation to celebrate your freedom, once this damn thing is over?

Some people believe that if they hire a hugely expensive attorney with years of experience, they are going to achieve a result that will get them far more than they would have gotten through mediation or a reasonable negotiation. Perhaps, if you are worth $500 million, it makes sense to spend some of that fortune in the hope of a better result. For the other 99.9% of us, it does not make any sense.

You will doubtless hear endless stories of what a great settlement this or that person achieved because their attorney was a genius, or the other lawyer was bamboozled, or whatever the fantasy may be. But any ethical and experienced divorce attorney will tell you that it is just not so. Show them your Financial Affidavit (we will get to that soon), give them the critical information about the marriage (i.e., length of marriage, number and ages of children, assets brought into the marriage by each party, whether you have a prenuptial agreement, and so forth) and within an incredibly narrow band they will predict the outcome. It is not a party trick or a magic act, it is simply how the law works. Do not be fooled into spending large sums of money to achieve what any decent family law practitioner could have foreseen at the outset.

So, what are these considerations that will affect the financial terms in a divorce? Each state has its own statutory list of factors to be considered, but we will simplify that here, setting out the key terms that essentially apply everywhere. It may seem like a long list, but do not let your eyes glaze over, and do not fail to study these elements. When you read it through, you will see it is generally governed by common sense:

a) The duration of the marriage and the age and health of both parties (this is a huge factor!)

b) The need of either party to occupy or own the Marital Home and a fair division of the contents

c) The loss to either party of inheritance or pension rights upon divorce

d) Any claim one spouse may have to marital property where their name does not appear on the title (e.g., the two of you own a vacation home, but the deed was only in one of your names)

e) Any claim one spouse may have to the increase in value of property owned by the other spouse, where that increase is partly the result of the other spouse furthering the career or career potential of the other party (e.g., one party works so the other can get an advanced degree, or become a doctor, or whatever, you will see an example of that under the Mediation section)

f) The liquid or non-liquid character of all marital property (e.g., sometimes things cannot be easily divided, such as a valuable painting, or sometimes an asset does not have an obvious market value, such as minority ownership in a small business, which is also covered in (j), below)

g) The probable future financial circumstances of each party (i.e., one spouse has a much larger earning potential than the other, such as a doctor and nurse divorcing, which will affect the alimony amount)

h) The educational background and degree status of each party

i) The past and present job experience of each party

j) The impossibility or difficulty of evaluating any component, asset or any interest in a business, corporation or profession; and the economic desirability of retaining such asset or interest intact and free from any claim or interference by any other party

k) The present and past incomes of each party during the term of the marriage from any and every source, subject to each party having fully disclosed these to the other party and each warranting and guaranteeing to the other that he or she had not concealed anything from the other party

l) The property of the respective parties, including but not limited to, marital property distributed between the parties during the course of the marriage, and personal or real property exchanged or given as gifts to each other or sold to each other during the course of the marriage, and personal or real property received by the respective parties from third parties by gift, bequest, devise or otherwise

m) The present and future capacity for each party to become or to remain self-supporting

n) The standard of living during the marriage

o) The tax consequences to each party

p) The wasteful dissipation of family assets by either spouse, if any (e.g., a gambling spouse who frittered away their savings)

q) The time and training necessary to enable the Husband or the Wife to become self-supporting (in the event of a non-working spouse)

r) The nature and extent of existing health and life insurance and the contemplated need for same in the future

We recognize that you might find this a daunting list, but let's take a step back and see what it is really about—common sense. Length of the marriage, and the ages, health, education, occupations and earning potential of the parties are all obvious factors in figuring out who gets what in a divorce. As for the more esoteric items, such as the liquidity of certain assets, the contributions made by each spouse and tax consequences are also reasonable. Now ask yourself, what factors are *not* on the list?

Who cheated? Who lied? Who was abusive? Who was mean, sexually withholding, or otherwise the villain of your personal drama? Notice that none of those things are to be considered by the court in resolving the financial arrangements. The only thing that comes close to that sort of subjective test is the mention of a "wasteful dissipation" of family assets, just in case one party is gambling away—or giving away—the family loot.

Courts in some states will take notice of who caused the failure of the marriage, if the actions are especially offensive, but except in extraordinary circumstances, the results are unlikely to be modified by much. In the typical breakup, where both sides share some portion of the blame, rely on the list above for guidance.

We are not trying to provide a legal education or ask you to analyze these various terms like an expert. What we want you to see is that the breakup of a marriage ultimately becomes a clinical measure of different elements that lead to a formula for the division of property and debts, and provisions for support. The point, as suggested above, is that once a good lawyer has your financial data, then within a reasonable degree of certainty:

HE OR SHE SHOULD BE ABLE TO APPLY THIS MATRIX TO YOUR SITUATION AND PREDICT THE RESULT.

In the next chapter, we will discuss how to select a lawyer, and Rule One should be their ability to provide this analysis. If they tell you they cannot, start looking for another lawyer.

But first, we need to do some more homework.

Financials

Before you, or your lawyer, can begin the process of assessing your situation and determining how your assets need to be divided, you will need to create a financial summary for the two of you to review.

Some people find this easy, others not so much. We have known spouses—unfortunately it is often the wife, and that is not a sexist judgment, just a fact—who plead ignorance when it comes to the economics of their marriage. Others say, "He handles all of our investments." Or "My wife always pays the bills." Or "I live on an allowance. My spouse takes care of the money." Or "I just sign the tax return every year. I don't really know what my spouse earns."

And so on.

Even if some or all of that is true for you, it is no excuse for you not to be able to put together the numbers you will need. This is war, information is power, and you must do the work required to pull all this data together.

Your Financial Statement, or Financial Affidavit as it is often called, is not complicated.

It has just a few sections that need to be filled out:

1. Income

In this section, you should list all income earned by you and your spouse, as well as any unearned income (such as dividends, interest and so forth.) This can be obtained from your annual income tax returns. If you do not have them, go find them and take photocopies of the last three years' filings. If you cannot find them, but you and your spouse filed jointly as a married couple—which people generally do since it saves taxes—then call the accountant. He is legally obligated to give you copies since you were a signatory.

2. Expenses

This is nothing more than a laundry list of what you spend every month. Mortgage or rent. Utilities, such as gas, electric, oil, and water. Food, restaurants, dry cleaners, car payments, gasoline, hair salons—all of the real costs of living. Some of these things will not be payable monthly, such as insurance on your cars or home. Just get the number and divide it, so if you pay semi-annually you divide by 6, if you pay quarterly you divide by 3 and if you pay once a year you divide by 12. Simple. The key is not to leave anything out. Vacations, birthday and holiday gifts, things that do not immediately come to mind. Look into your checkbook and credit card statements for the past year. What you want to create is an accurate picture of what it costs you to live now, so you can determine what it will cost after the split. The simplest way to do this is to take your most recent three or more months of bank and credit card statements and see how your money was spent.

3. Liabilities

Simply list everything you and your spouse owe, including credit card debt, the balance of your mortgage and anything left on your car note.

4. Assets

This is the flip side of liabilities—the value of your home (start with a fair estimate, you may need an appraisal later), the value of your car, jewelry, artwork, vacation homes and anything else you own that has financial value.

Following is a simple form of Financial Affidavit. You can add or delete categories to suit your situation and, when you are done, the importance of this document cannot be overstated. This is the information from which an experienced lawyer can make that prediction of how your case will end up. It will also provide you a snapshot of your economic status—what you will need to live going forward and how your assets and liabilities should be fairly split.

FINANCIAL AFFIDAVIT

I. INCOME

Gross Weekly Salary
Federal Withholding
CT Withholding
Medicare
Social Security
Annuities
Interest and Dividends
NET MONTHLY INCOME

II. EXPENSES

Mortgage
Real Estate taxes
Heat
Water
Electric
Internet
Telephone
Refuse removal
Cable TV
Yard maintenance and plantings
Security System
Household Repairs
Food
Restaurants
Clothing (self)
Clothing (children)
Dry cleaning, laundry, tailor
Medical/Dental Expenses
(Including children)
Child Education
Tuition
Room and Board
Other expenses
Entertainment
(Including children)

Pet Care
Automobile
    Lease payments
    Repairs
    Gas and Oil
    Car wash
Gifts
    Holidays
    Birthdays
Charities
Vacations

TOTAL MONTHLY EXPENSES

III. LIABILITIES	Original Debt	Current Payment	Weekly Balance
Credit Cards			
Store Charges			

TOTAL LIABILITIES

IV. ASSETS	Value	Debt	Equity
Real Estate			
Personal Property			
Furniture and personal property			
Automobiles:			
Jewelry			
Bank Accounts			
Stocks and Bonds			
Insurance			

TOTAL ASSETS

SUMMARY

TOTAL WEEKLY INCOME	$	TOTAL VALUE OF ASSETS	$
TOTAL WEEKLY EXPENSES	$	TOTAL LIABILITIES	$

CERTIFICATION

I hereby certify that the foregoing statement is true and accurate to the best of my knowledge and belief.

Signed: __________________________

At this point, you have a list of the basic terms that are considered by a court—and lawyers—in hammering out a verdict at trial or a financial agreement. You have also created a statement of your income, expenses, assets, and liabilities that will be used to determine a fair and legal outcome. Now it is time to choose the vehicle that will get you where you want to go— Splitsville!

4.1 Negotiation between the parties

We like to call this the "kitchen table settlement." Yes, we know, the two of you hate each other, one of you doesn't trust the other—or neither of you trusts the other—and there is no way you're going to sit down and reach an agreement on all of the complicated issues that need to be addressed in a divorce—splitting assets, support payments, visitation, who gets the house, who gets the car and who gets Buffy the cat. He is a controlling bastard; she is a selfish bitch and there is no way you will ever reach a compromise. However, just in case the level of acrimony is not already nuclear, this is an incredibly practical and inexpensive way out of the marriage. No one knows your finances and personalities better than the two of you, so maybe it is worth trying. In one of my favorite divorces, the husband came to me with eight single-spaced pages setting out the division of every single asset, right down to the forks and knives, including visitation and child support, living arrangements and anything else one could think of in a marital dissolution. It had been a tempestuous marriage, he was a martinet, and she was a lunatic, but they were determined not to let other people guide their destiny. The husband told me to incorporate everything in that list into a formal separation agreement and his wife would give it to an attorney to review, which I did. They were divorced in no time and remain friends to this day, their daughters having enjoyed the collateral benefit of this amicable process.

My favorite divorce

I have handled some tough divorces, some nasty divorces and some relatively easy cases.

I've also had my share of notable clients along the way. I represented a famous television star who had more money than you could give away in a lifetime, but insisted on wreaking vengeance on her philandering husband, and I could not blame her. Then there was a famous NBA star who was one of the greatest gentlemen I've ever known, who insisted on giving his wife far more than she would have been entitled to at trial simply because he wanted his children to be comfortable and because he still loved her. He just could not bear to live with her anymore.

But those cases do not compare with the matter I handled for a doctor I knew.

He and his wife were both highly intelligent, professionally accomplished and emotionally as mismatched as the proverbial oil and water. I was acquainted with both of them, liked each of them, and had wondered how they ever managed to stay married as long as they did—other than for the benefit of their two terrific sons.

But the concept of "staying together for the children" in a bad marriage is not usually a great idea, as we discuss elsewhere in this book. They ultimately reached a breaking point, mutually deciding it was time to split.

Given the volatility of their relationship, one could have reasonably expected a knock-down, drag-out divorce. They were famous for their public spats and her temper was nothing less than volcanic.

But reason prevailed. Among their other personality traits, it is not too much to say that both of them were rather careful about their money. Whatever differences they had; they were determined not to enrich some lawyers when they could sort things out for themselves.

As a result, they became authors of one of the greatest kitchen table settlements I have ever witnessed. (I actually owe the expression, kitchen table settlement, to their case, since that is literally what occurred. They sat down in their kitchen with pads, pens and a laptop and proceeded to list every asset they held—I'm talking about every knife, fork, and crystal tumbler— then divided everything, taking turns when it came to paintings, china and so on.) They addressed their debts, which consisted primarily of the mortgage on their home, and the issue of who would live where. They discussed what they should do about their sons completing their high school educations and where everyone should live.

I was not in the loop for any of this and can therefore take no credit. The first I heard of it was when the doctor called and asked to see me. He arrived for our meeting with two copies of twelve single-spaced pages. He handed one to me, explained what it was and asked me to prepare a separation and property settlement agreement that would incorporate all the terms they had set out, and then to get him a divorce.

The thoroughness of the document was astounding, and I told him so. I also advised that there were a couple of necessary steps to getting this done, which I promised to keep as simple as possible. First, I explained that the court would require that he and his wife each complete a financial affidavit fully disclosing to the other all that each of them knew of the assets and debts they were splitting, as well as their respective incomes and expenses. As expected, he found this an annoying piece of business, but understood it was a legal requirement and said he would get right to it, so I provided him the form. The second item was legal representation for his wife.

Although he insisted that they both trusted me and were willing to allow me to handle everything, I explained it was not possible. Not only would the court want her to have her own lawyer, given the amount of assets involved, but I explained that the agreement could be challenged in the future on the grounds that the parties were not represented by independent counsel when they signed the agreement.

His wife went to a lawyer friend who agreed to review their twelve-page list, the agreement I would prepare based on the terms they had enumerated, would assist her with the financial affidavit and then attend the brief hearing for the uncontested divorce (which is where both sides agree they want the marriage terminated by the court.)

It all went as smoothly as one could want. Neither I nor the other attorney saw any reason to challenge any part of the resolution they reached, it seemed fair in all respects. We got the required paperwork done for the court and in short order scheduled our appearance in court.

Perhaps the best part of all this was the day of that hearing. We told the judge how this had developed, and he went to great lengths to congratulate the parties on their wisdom before bringing the gavel down on their marriage. The four of us left the courthouse together and, out on the street, the doctor asked us to wait for a moment before we parted. He went to his car, came back with a camera, and asked if we would take a couple of photos of his wife and him in front of the building. The other attorney and I exchanged curious glances, to which my client said, "We have pictures from the day we married, why not for the day we got divorced?"

Among the many benefits of their incredibly sane approach to the end of their marriage, I would like to note a few. They have remained friends to this day, which is now many years later. They spent almost nothing on legal fees. Their sons are bright, happy, successful, and well-adjusted. Both young men maintain close and loving relationships with both parents—the four of them often share holidays together.

I am not saying you will be this fortunate as you travel the road to Splitsville, but I ask that you at least keep this in mind when you consider your vehicle.

4.2 Collaboration

Collaboration is very much in vogue, but we begin with the warning that is it not something we generally advise. Let's first describe how it works, then we can discuss the pluses and minuses.

Collaboration is an odd hybrid, where you each get an attorney who promises to play nice in trying to hammer out a settlement. It is agreed at the outset that, should you not reach terms, you will then choose another of the paths described below, with new lawyers. The idea is that the lawyers you choose to collaborate through should have no motivation to create strife or conflict. Their only goal should be compromise. Failing that, they will be replaced.

The view here is that it will generally be a waste of time and money, with a few exceptions.

If your assets are substantial and/or complicated, it may be worthwhile to engage in this process. Having attorneys review and advise how to handle these things may be useful, along with the assistance of accountants experienced in this area. Knowledgeable lawyers who are committed to a non-confrontational approach can be valuable in such circumstances. This is particularly true if the marital estate involves trusts; real estate holdings other than the marital home; a varied stock and bond portfolio; ownership interests in one or more companies where the value needs to be independently ascertained; and so forth.

As stated above, the key here is to be sure the attorneys you choose have agreed to exit stage right if the collaboration fails. Most attorneys, by nature and training, are invested in proving how smart and tough they are, so finding the right fit for a collaboration will be important.

I just know he is going to take advantage of me!

Felicia is an exceedingly bright woman who married Greg, an exceptionally intelligent man. As a result of his intellect and skills, Greg built an investment business with a number of affiliates and subsidiaries. They became quite wealthy, which was wonderful, but which also had certain unintended consequences. The most important of those was the decision for Felicia to become a housewife and mother, rather than pursuing the career in advertising she had when they met. Given her talents and creative spirit, this turned out to be a mistake. Over time, Felicia began to feel unfulfilled, bored, and underappreciated at home. As her children got older, they obviously needed her less, and she felt a growing lack of respect from Greg.

This is a plight faced by many women who choose homemaking over an outside profession, but in Felicia's case it was eased in large part by their luxurious lifestyle. At least for a while. Ultimately the emotional negatives outweighed the affluent trappings, and the marriage fractured. Greg found women he thought more interesting because they were in the business world, and he strayed. Felicia sought comfort elsewhere and was also unfaithful. Their split ultimately was not about hate, it was about a woman who had not realized her potential—a very sad circumstance indeed.

When it became clear there was no way to rebuild the love and trust and attraction that had brought them together, they agreed divorce was inevitable. Neither wanted to engage in a bitter fight. They wanted to preserve their relationships with the children. There were certainly enough assets for everyone to be comfortable. And so, they agreed to work out a fair settlement on their own.

When Felicia sought counsel, it was not with a view toward breaching that purpose. It was because she felt at an enormous disadvantage in discussing their finances.

Greg was the earner. In addition to running his business enterprises, he had always paid their bills and handled their personal investments. Even when Felicia was working, her long suit had been creativity, not accounting. And now she feared that she would not be her husband's equal in their negotiations. Having heard about collaboration, she wanted to know if that was the right way to go.

In the case of Felicia and Greg, collaboration made sense. Despite the mutual infidelity and the resultant unhappiness, they were committed to avoiding a legal battle. Interestingly, Greg initially opposed the idea, which only increased his wife's concern that he might not deal fairly with her as the marital estate was divided. He resisted the prospect of having her attorney and forensic accountants delving into his records and holdings, claiming that there were numerous and complex transactions that might unravel if exposed to the light of day. Then he played the "tax card," expressing concern that opening up his books might expose them to tax liabilities he had carefully and legally avoided.

It was a clever argument, but total hogwash. If his transactions were legal, there was no reason to fear an audit, and the more complicated he insisted they were the more reason for his wife to get help.

This was a situation where collaboration worked. After getting past those preliminary objections, Greg lawyered up, his assets were examined and an equitable arrangement was reached.

If you believe there is a path to a peaceful resolution of the issues in your divorce— finances, custody, visitation—but you suspect your spouse has more information about your holdings; or you do not fully understand the extent or details of the marital estate; or you would just generally feel better having a professional ride shotgun during the process, then you can make collaboration work. Just remember our initial caveat—this is a process that takes sincere intention from both of you to reach a fair accord. If this is just going to be a game one of you is going to play, save the money and move on to another vehicle.

4.3 Mediation

Mediation is becoming an increasingly popular means of settling divorce cases and, if the two of you cannot do it on your own, we are big fans of this option rather than engaging in collaboration. The essence of this process is the involvement of an independent third-party to hear from both sides and suggest a solution, so it is critical that you select a mediator with lots of experience. This is one area about which you can ask friends (despite the warnings in the next chapter) looking for those who have been through the process or know someone who has. You can also check online to see who is available in your area, leaning toward retired judges or retired attorneys who specialized in family law.

The way this works is fairly simple. Either with or without attorneys, you each prepare a financial statement setting out all of your assets, liabilities, income, and expenses (we will discuss these "Financial Statements" elsewhere in the book.) You can do this together, which is best, or you can each prepare your own. Each of you then puts together your wish list of what you think a settlement should look like. All of this is submitted to the mediator in advance for her or him to consider before your meeting occurs.

We favor full day mediations where enough time is set aside to go back and forth like Henry Kissinger doing shuttle diplomacy, the mediator going through everything in an effort to bring the parties to terms. Again, whether you bring attorneys is optional, although we feel that if one side insists on having a lawyer, then both sides should be represented. Mediations are not binding, which means that the mediator has no right to issue a decision or compel a result. The mediator's role is to try and pull the parties toward some center line so that an agreement can be reached that is satisfactory to both sides.

The success rate of mediations is very high, the process far less expensive than contested litigation and, with a good mediator, the vitriol between the parties is generally reduced along the way. A variation here would be for the parties to agree in advance that, in the event they failed to come to an agreement, the mediator would have the ability to issue a binding decision, but we certainly do not favor that notion. If you really cannot come to terms after a full day with the help of an experienced professional, you may need to move on to the more contentious options below.

Mediation is a fairly simple process that is sometimes misunderstood, causing people to resist the idea. Simply stated, mediation is a form of negotiation that is moderated by an individual mutually chosen by you and your spouse. It is generally scheduled for a set period of time—a specified number of hours or, in some cases, a full day (which can often run into the evening.) The key is to have the parties focus in on reaching an agreement in that limited time frame, so the negotiation does not drag on and on.

In order to accomplish this, there is work to be done before the mediation occurs. A good mediator will require that each of the parties submit certain basic information, usually consisting of:

1. A brief summary of your personal information, including the length of your marriage, ages of you and your spouse, your educations, work history, where you live, any secondary homes, the ages of any children, and so forth.
2. A financial statement (which you have already created.) This is critical information for the mediator since it will provide the data upon which they will propose a settlement.
3. A simple statement of what result you would like to see in the divorce—how you would like to divide the assets and liabilities and what payments there might be for your spouse or you, and for your children.

Once the mediator has all of this from both of you, he or she will take time to analyze the data and may even ask for additional input. Once that is done, the date for the mediation will be set.

You and your spouse can attend the mediation with or without lawyers. It is a bad idea for one of you to have an attorney and the other not. As much as we want to reduce your expenses throughout the divorce process, we must also concede that your chances of reaching an agreement at a mediation will be enhanced if you both have legal representation present. The reason for this is simple—the mediator will make certain proposals based on what each of you have asked for in your respective "wish list" of terms. Neither of you will get everything you want, but having a lawyer there to advise you will help provide guidance as to whether the proposed settlement terms are reasonable. Most important, your attorney should be able to tell you if the settlement is likely to be close to what you would receive if you spent a small fortune—or large fortune—taking the case to trial. It is also more probable, with attorneys present, that the details of an agreement can be hammered out then and there.

It is critical to understand what a mediation is not because these misconceptions sometimes cause people to reject the process. It is not binding arbitration. It is not a trial. The mediator has no authority to impose her will or opinions on you. If you choose a mediator with lots of experience in the field of matrimonial law—which is the only type you should select—their advice will be invaluable in moving you and your spouse toward a resolution that will resemble the result you would get after a costly and stressful trial. That is the reason to mediate and that is why it is a favored option.

In some of the most difficult cases we have handled, mediation was successful, often to our amazement. If the mediator and your respective lawyers are experienced and have real integrity, there is no reason why you should not come away with an agreement you and your spouse can live with into the future.

The Wicked Witch of the East

I have certainly met some surly characters in my career, but none of them hold a candle to Eileen. By all accounts, her husband Frank was a devoted husband and father. He was a good provider, as the expression goes, was loyal and honest and tried hard to make his marriage work.

Eileen, however, came from a long line of divorced relatives, most notably a mother who became an avowed man-hater when her husband walked out, imbuing her only child with as much poison as she could inject into her system.

When Frank came to me, he was beside himself with emotional pain. He and Eileen argued frequently, almost always initiated by her as I learned from others who knew them. She had asked him to leave on several occasions, which he would do, only to return in the hope of working things out. But this time, he explained, was too much. She had told both him and his college-age son to leave the house on Christmas Eve. She was on one of her notorious rants, and insisted they get out of "her" house or she would call the police.

This time, Frank told me, he was not going back.

Eileen lawyered up, blamed Frank for the split, and demanded everything they owned as her proposed settlement. Worse than that, she forbid her high school aged daughter to even speak with her father.

As it happened, she chose a lawyer with real integrity, who quickly got a sense of who his client was, a helpful development in a tough situation. Frank was heartbroken over the forced rift with his daughter. He did not care if Eileen kept the marital home or the fact that he would be paying her support for many years to come. He loved his daughter and wanted more than anything to heal the vicious wounds his wife was inflicting on their relationship.

The best way to bring an end to this melodrama, both Eileen's lawyer and I agreed, was a full-day mediation with a top-notch mediator. We had some difficulty getting Eileen to agree to anyone I would consent to, but we finally settled on a retired lawyer with over 50 years of matrimonial practice. He was a no-nonsense guy with a grandfatherly affect and an incredibly sharp mind.

I could regale you with any number of stories about the ten hours we spent negotiating that day, but my favorite was when Eileen started cursing at me across the conference table. The mediator put an immediate stop to that and asked Eileen's attorney and me to have a private discussion with him. In another room, Eileen's lawyer was the first to speak.

"My client is a bitch."

The mediator smiled. "Yes, she is, but this is not my first rodeo. Why don't you two sit back and let me do my job."

We agreed and do his job he did.

The mediator spoke for over an hour, without interruption. He laid out the hazards of litigation, the way the law works and the predictable result in their case. He also pointed out the possibility that a judge might be swayed in one direction or another if he felt a party was being unreasonable, the message not lost on Eileen. She was repulsive, not stupid. She knew her demands were ridiculous, not to mention the dangers inherent in a judge being confronted with evidence of how she was working to damage Frank's relationship with his daughter.

He then spoke with Frank and me alone, followed by a private session with Eileen and her counsel. After more back and forth we had a settlement, and no one was more surprised than I. Before the mediation, Frank asked me what I thought about our chances of reaching a compromise.

"About ten percent," I told him, "but it's worth the shot."

It is difficult to predict what might turn a mediation from a confrontation to a settlement.

In this case, a large factor was Eileen's selfish and destructive behavior toward her own daughter. She had enough self-awareness to realize she could not have that behavior exposed in a courtroom, where her own son was prepared to tell the truth of what his mother was doing to his sister.

The sad postscript is that Eileen's poison continues to infect her daughter. Years later, she will not speak with her father, which remains the heartache of his life. On the other hand, he has left behind a cruel partner, has found a mate he loves and, other than the ongoing hope he may someday reconcile with his daughter, he is a very happy man.

Part of that is his decision to never speak with or communicate with Eileen again. I have the pleasure of periodic emails from her, all of which are nasty, and all of which are about support payments, which Frank makes on time—in his words, a small price to pay to be rid of her.

<u>You can't win 'em all.</u>

Sally and Bob came to me for mediation. From the outset they made two critical mistakes I could not talk them out of, largely because I had been highly recommended and they were looking for a miracle rather than a resolution. First, they did not want to hire their own attorneys, they wanted me to handle the entire thing. Second, they were convinced this would take multiple sessions, rather than committing to a one-day marathon of negotiations.

As I say, I counseled them to reconsider their approach, but they were convinced that they needed to pursue this course, so I did my best. The problems I faced were interesting.

Sally was a delightful woman, a so-called "stay at home mom" who could be the poster girl for OCD. To say she ran her household like a military operation would do General Patton proud. Among other things, she kept a calendar for Bob, their two children and herself that ran six months into the future. It was one of those Outlook calendars, a month to a page, with each of the four family members had his or her own color. The activities included everything you could imagine, such as school, music lessons, sporting events and social dates for her son and daughter. Work, social gatherings and even down time for Bob and her. The detail was mind-boggling, but she believed this was the only way to conduct a disciplined and useful life.

Bob was her polar opposite. He was a successful money manager who had a laid-back attitude for someone advising his clients about tens of millions of dollars in investments. It was clear from the outset that he found his wife's micro-management of their time annoying and had reached the point where he could not deal with it anymore.

And then there was the affair.

It was revealed, in our first session, that Bob had engaged in an extra-marital relationship with a young woman he met through business, which Sally was not willing to forgive.

Given their respective positions, divorce was inevitable and, it seemed to me, the financial arrangements should be fairly simple to resolve. They had been married more than twenty years, had started with very little and there was no prenuptial agreement, which generally leads to an even division of the assets. They did not seem to have any disagreement over visitation and child support, Bob was willing to let Sally keep the marital home as part of the arrangement, and he was prepared to do whatever was necessary to provide for their children's college and graduate school. That left only one issue, the amount of support for Sally.

In session after session, I laid out the calculations a court would use in the event of a trial. I explained, in repetitive detail, what the overall economic arrangements would ultimately be if left to the court to decide. I warned them against spending all of the fees that would be involved in a contested trial, not to mention the upset for both of them and their children. Yet, no matter how many ways I came at this, every one of our hour-long sessions would end with Sally scolding her husband for ruining their marriage by his unfaithful conduct and Bob, after sitting through these attacks, ultimately getting up and leaving—with the assurance we would try again next week.

After a couple of months of these weekly diatribes, Sally called me one afternoon and asked if she could stop by. I told her that I did not want to discuss anything about the case without Bob, present, but she told me not to be concerned. She arrived with a large plate of homemade chocolate chip cookies and a simple announcement.

"I know how hard you tried, and I appreciate all you've done, but I just cannot let him get away with being the philandering piece of shit he is." Then she told me she was hiring one of the most expensive lawyers in the area.

I received a call from Bob, about a year and a half later, telling me that they were finally divorced. He thanked me for my efforts and told me, "To your credit, the result at trial was almost exactly what you predicted in all those meetings. Except," he added, "that between the two of us we spent over $150,000 in legal fees."

Ugh!

Not every mediation is successful, of course, but the case of Sally and Bob was programmed for failure at the start. The first mistake was that Sally saw our sessions as an opportunity to repeatedly bash her husband, calling him everything from a sonofabitch to a cheating scumbag. Was Bob wrong? Of course, he was. He had clearly abandoned the marriage long before and only put up with her anger in the hope they could wrap things up and move on. He was willing to take responsibility for destroying the marriage—even if there was more to it than that—but his *mea culpa* was not enough for her. She wanted blood.

The second mistake was their insistence that we drag out these discussions over numerous weeks. If they had followed my advice, we might have had a twelve-hour marathon of upset, vitriol and apologies, but they both may have run out of steam and reached an accord.

Instead, they dragged each other through a nasty trial, their children along with it, and any chance of a civil relationship in the future as the parents of those children was lost forever.

So, what is the lesson here? If your marriage is over, find a better way to deal with your upset than continually returning to the source of your problems, as if the spouse you now want to be rid of will somehow provide a path to moving forward toward happiness.

4.4 Negotiation between attorneys

You cannot stand each other. Reaching an amicable settlement between the two of you is an impossibility. Collaboration was a bust; or you cannot agree on an independent mediator, not even with the help of your lawyers; or the mediation was a flop. So, what's next?

Now you're going to let your attorneys duke it out, let them do the fighting for you as the clock ticks on their hourly fees.

The legal profession can be noble, helpful, even necessary. But when it comes to divorce there is an inherent problem we have already alluded to in this book. There is an inherent conflict between the professional and the person they represent.

Lawyers are, after all, businessmen and businesswomen. They are in the game to earn money, and the more the better. The greater the problems between you and your spouse, the more time that needs to be spent resolving issues, the larger their fees. In other words, they have no profit motive to reach a quick and fair resolution. Their interests are served by filing motions, demanding to review more and more documents from the other side, and negotiating your case to the bitter end.

This is not to say that most divorce lawyers are unethical, quite the contrary. But some cannot help themselves. Some convince themselves they are doing what is best for you. They will tell you they need to pore through ten years of tax returns, three years of credit card bills and have every possession in your marital life appraised. Some will tell you, "It would be malpractice for me not to complete a thorough due diligence of your marital finances," and they will mean it when they say it.

But hold on here. With rare exception, who knows your finances better than you and your spouse? Oh sure, there are situations where one of you has a Swiss bank account you're hiding, or undisclosed investments, or a business that must be properly valued. Even in those circumstances, however, there is no need for that to become anyone's life work, right? More to the point, there is no reason to pay the lawyers on both sides to be involved in those squabbles.

Just agree to an independent party to review these things and establish their value.

We concede, with all of the warnings we are giving here, that negotiations through attorneys is the classic means of reaching an agreement. It also tends to be far more expensive and upsetting than a mediation, for obvious reasons. The longer the case takes, the more motions filed, the more appearances in court and the more complex negotiations, the more money they make. Divorce cases are just like any other case to the attorney handling it. It is a source of business and income, and when it is over in most cases the lawyer will never see you again.

Unless, of course, you happen to repeat your mistakes. The best matrimonial attorney I know in my area drives a Rolls-Royce. What else do you need to know? That is not to say there are not terrific lawyers out there who work for you, fight for you, and try and get you the best deal possible. But as you will see, when we discuss THE TRUTH ABOUT WHAT WILL HAPPEN, it really matters who represents you since the likely result in your case will be within a very narrow band of a much larger spectrum. People shooting for the moon in a divorce should join NASA, because that is as close as they're going to come. Reality will ultimately dictate how the case turns out and any good lawyer can tell you within an hour of meeting you and listening to your situation and financial picture, where that result will wind up.

<u>Sometimes it just takes the right lawyer—on the other side!</u>

Blake and Teresa were in the middle of an especially nasty divorce, with a lot of assets at stake. One might think, with all the money and property they owned, that reaching a settlement would be easy. There was enough for everyone, including the children, but that did not matter.

The financial aspects of their split became a battleground where they could play out all of the things they had come to despise about each other.

Not a happy picture, and not inclined to foster reasonable compromises.

Add to this conflict Teresa's law firm. It was one of those huge outfits where the reception area in their high-rise headquarters was large enough to comfortably house a family of five. They never did anything without involving a partner, at least one associate and a paralegal who would keep the minutes of every discussion, meeting, and court appearance. That meant their hourly rate was a combined fortune, and there was no motivation to bring the case to a close any time soon. If Teresa was happy paying for endless sessions where you got to bash her husband—occasions that took place both in and out of his presence—then who were they to deny her?

Once again, we want to make clear that we do not think most matrimonial attorneys are evil, but we acknowledge that self-interest is difficult to avoid. If Teresa's lawyers did not provide what she wanted, she could take her marbles and go somewhere else, so why not make her happy for the moment—even if it was doing long-term damage for her prospects for a better future, her relationship with her children and so forth.

Any number of attempts were made to bring a measure of reason to the negotiations, all to no avail. The nature of the differences between Blake and Teresa became increasingly unimportant. Hate, rage, resentment—these were the emotions that ruled the day.

Until another attorney entered the scene.

Ironically, it was Teresa and not Blake who brought in a hired gun to assist. We shall call him Brian. By reputation, Brian is one of the top and toughest divorce lawyers in the area, and Teresa wanted to turn up the temperature on her husband. What she and her lawyers did not know, however, was that her new champion happened to have an excellent history with Blake's lawyer. They had worked together on another large case and shared a mutual sense of respect. And that turned the tide.

A conference was arranged, ostensibly for the purpose of showing off Teresa's new guy, and Brian played his part to perfection. He sneered and threatened and dominated the conversation for well over an hour, all to the delight of his new client. Then he called for a break so the attorneys could speak privately. Brian insisted that only Blake's lawyer and Teresa's lead counsel could attend, leaving the big firm associates and paralegal behind to twiddle their thumbs and take notes.

In a separate conference room, Teresa's original counsel was treated to stories about how Brian and Blake's lawyer had met. Brian recounted how they had resolved a case that made the millions involved in the current case look like chicken feed. Then, after a bit of sociable catching-up, he turned to Blake's lawyer and asked, "What is it going to take to settle this case?"

An hour later, after some back and forth and a lot more reminiscing, Brian announced that they had a deal Teresa would be a fool not to accept. That was followed by a private consultation among Brian, Teresa and her big firm counsel, who had been rendered virtually speechless, for her to be convinced the terms that had been reached were as good as it was going to get. In the end, she was, and then paid Brian a sizeable bonus for working out a deal she could have easily had a year before—and before over a million dollars in legal fees had been wasted.

The point is obvious—be sure your lawyer(s) are working for your benefit, not just to please you for the moment as they run up the costs of unnecessary strife. You may hate your spouse, but no one knows your financial and personal circumstances better that you do. Please remember, one of the goals of this book is to help you get to Splitsville without making your lawyer rich.

4.5 Trial

Contested litigation is the final lifeline of a drowning man or woman. Whatever your circumstances, if you end up here, paying lawyers untold sums of money and leaving your future to a judge who neither knows you nor has any particular stake in what happens to you, then we are sorry you were unable to get to a successful finish through collaboration, negotiation or mediation. As they say about embarking on a path of revenge, first dig two graves.

In spite of the hazards of litigation, let us begin by being fair to the lawyers and judges. Most attorneys will work hard to achieve the best result possible for you. Most are intelligent, experienced and do not want to fail. Regardless of their view of your case, losing at trial is not good for their reputation, so expect them to fight it out.

Judges are generally overworked, underpaid and many have developed a cynical outer skin from having been exposed to so many contentious spouses, combative attorneys, and fact patterns that would make television writers blush. On top of that, they are constrained by the rule of law which means, in effect, that even if they think something might be fair, they may not be able to render that judgment because of the limits on their authority.

One example should suffice to make this conundrum clear.

Whose money is it?

Serena was anything but serene. If there was ever a name that did not suit someone, well, you get the idea.

In fairness, she had a right to be angry. Her husband, Pierre, had left her for an extremely wealthy woman who apparently found his French-American charm irresistible. And when we say, "he left her," we mean just that. He walked out on Serena, walked out on their children, walked out on his interior design business, left Serena without enough money to cover next month's utilities, and took up his new life as a kept man in a luxurious mansion with a chauffeured limousine, a maid, cook and butler, and the obligatory vacation home in the Caribbean.

Not only that, but he also made it clear that just as soon as he could get a divorce decree, he was going to marry his new love.

Why mention this case here? It was obvious that he was a selfish jerk. Whoever or whatever Serena had been during their marriage, certainly his young children did not deserve this, right? The court would take care of the obvious inequities here. How could they not?

We will explain how Pierre could live his opulent lifestyle while paying a minimal amount of child support and absolutely no alimony whatsoever.

It was because his new inamorata held all of the money and assets, and none of them belonged to him.

"But wait," you say. "The judge had to see how unfair this was. Surely, once the divorce was granted and he remarried, then things could be

equalized. After all, look at the lifestyle he was enjoying. Some of that had to be awarded to Serena and the kids."

Wrong. Even after Pierre married Miss Moneybags, Serena and his children had no right to any of her money, which she and Pierre certainly thought to be the right decision. It turns out that "Lifestyle" is not a legal measure by which child and spousal support can be measured. Just because Pierre remarried, his wife's money did not become his.

"But wait," you say again. "Was there no obligation that he worked to help support the children?"

Good question, and this time you are correct. The trouble is, you cannot force anyone to work any particular job or seek any specified income. Pierre was an interior designer and, as such, pursued that career in the most listless, lackluster, unsuccessful manner possible.

Pierre, to his credit, did make an offer to settle the case. It was not much, but he realized it was better than the result that awaited Serena if she went the whole route. But she was angry, felt betrayed, and was sure that justice would prevail—despite warnings from her lawyer about what would happen. No surprise, then, when the trial was a disaster for her. Since Pierre had no motive to settle, and since his attorney knew the law, it was left for the court to deliver the bad news. Even the judge expressed his frustration with the state of the law, while explaining there was nothing for him to do but base his decision on the paltry earnings Pierre had managed over the year since he split with Serena. He awarded no alimony and a pathetic sum for child support.

We acknowledge that this is an extreme case, but it does carry a point—do not think that a trial will yield some fair or just result for you. The law is the law, and it works in strange ways.

It will almost always be better for you to control your own destiny by making the best deal possible, then getting on with your journey to Splitsville.

4.6 Getting help from the court system itself

Believe it or not, there are actually times when the government bureaucracy can be useful and handling your own divorce can be one of those times. Most states offer forms from the court which allow you to file your own divorce action—without a lawyer! Many of those states even provide a mechanism for you to visit your local court and speak with a clerk who can guide you through the process.

For instance, in Connecticut you can get the help online, which you can follow up by visiting the court on line:

Filing for a Divorce without Children - CT Judicial Branch

www.jud.ct.gov › forms › grouped › family › divorce_...

Summons Family Actions (JD-FM-3) · Notice of Automatic Court Orders (JD-FM-158) ·

Motion for Orders Before Judgment (Pendente Lite) in Family Cases (JD-FM- ...

Filing for a Divorce with Children - CT Judicial Branch

www.jud.ct.gov › forms › grouped › family › divorce_...

For your final **divorce** hearing you have to fill out one of the following **forms** · Financial Affidavit (JD-FM-6) - Long · Financial Affidavit (JD-FM-6) - Short · Dissolution ...

Similarly, New York offers do-it-yourself options:

Uncontested Divorce - DIY Forms | NY CourtHelp

www.nycourts.gov › courthelp › diy › divorce

Mar 16, 2020 — The official home page of the **New York** State Unified **Court** System. We hear more than three million cases a year involving almost every type ...

Uncontested Divorce Overview · Children in a Divorce Case

DIY (Do-It-Yourself) Forms | NY CourtHelp - Unified Court ...

www.nycourts.gov › courthelp › diy

Case Type	Program	Court
Divorce	Uncontested Divorce	Supreme Court

Whatever State you reside in, a simple search online will provide the necessary information. This can be incredibly valuable for people who have already come to terms on their financial issues, and custody and visitation where appropriate. It can save you a lot of money in legal fees, and working together with your partner to get it done can sometimes become a surprising part of the healing process as well. Getting the papers filled out and filed can truly become the easiest part of your journey.

CHAPTER 5
SELECTING A LAWYER

"Divorce is a game played by lawyers." —Cary Grant

"Best Lawyer" lists make us laugh. What are they best at, exactly? Creating dissension between the parties? Inventing issues to prolong the case? Making themselves look smart while increasing the fees? Preparing endless motions and paperwork to show how smart they are, while you pay for the privilege of watching?

There is a matrimonial lawyer in our area who drives an extremely expensive car. So does his wife. Neither came from a wealthy family, nor did they win the lottery. He is a good lawyer, no denying that, but guess who paid for those automobiles, and the other lifestyle treasures they enjoy? People like you, people who were facing the end of their marriage and turned to the barracudas that troll the shallow waters of human misery.

Yes, I know that sounds harsh, but unfortunately it is true. These attorneys will justify what they do by claiming that their job is "getting the most they can" for their clients. Or "the best deal possible." Or, more candidly, "taking the other side to the cleaners."

But is any of that going to happen? Not really. Oh sure, some lawyers are better than others, smarter, more articulate, better negotiators, more experienced—but in the end, as we emphasize throughout this book, the results are always going to be within a thin band of the total spectrum of possible outcomes for which the law provides. There are gatekeepers appointed to prevent unjust outcomes—the judges who hear these cases every day and know where the final terms should end up.

You will hear stories from friends about how a great lawyer got so and so a fabulous settlement, or some moron representing their cousin got screwed by the other side. But in the end, if you drill down into the real facts, you will find that these tales are more about how those lawyers spin the facts after the deal is done, rather than about the actual terms.

You will also hear how some judge did the wrong thing, but that is almost always about a disappointed party who wanted or expected more than they were entitled to receive.

Do judges make mistakes? All the time. Are some lawyers better than others? Absolutely.

The key to a "successful result" is to be advised correctly on your particular case, not to hope that you are going to beat the system and reach terms that are unrealistically favorable to you.

So, how do you ensure you will receive the right advice?

To begin, you need to have a strategy in finding the right attorney for your case. Think about the lawyer you choose as the driver of the vehicle that will get you to Splitsville. Now envision the most perilous journey you will ever take, along winding mountain roads that have no guardrails and sheer cliffs on both sides. What qualities will you want in the person who is going to navigate that course?

You get the idea.

As much as we are opposed to you listening to cocktail party chatter about other divorces or allowing friends to sway your thinking one way or another, a recommendation from a trusted source about a decent lawyer is valuable. It is best, of course, if that source actually used that attorney, but word-of-mouth can be underrated. The important thing here is your own judgment, which should be based on a comprehensive interview.

Speaking with a lawyer for the first time is not unlike visiting a doctor. It can be intimidating. No matter how smart and successful you are, professionals know things you do not, and that can put you off. They speak a different language, have a different skill set, and that can set you on your heels.

DO NOT LET IT!

Remember this from the first meeting right through to the end game—THE LAWYER WORKS FOR YOU! He or she is providing a service for which you are paying, so do not be afraid to ask questions. Do not be afraid to look foolish if you need things explained more than once. Do not be afraid to question your attorney's advice, judgments, or actions.

But let's start with that first interview.

A lot of lawyers will make you feel as if they are interviewing you. They will ask for your story, which you are generally eager to share. They will write down all the details you provide, asking insightful questions that make you feel important—even intriguing—and in the end they will have controlled the narrative.

But wait. You're hiring them. Don't you want to know something about their background, skills, and attitudes? Of course, you do—or should—and that means you have to ask some very basic inquiries before you get too far into this new relationship. If you were hiring a plumbing contractor you would want to know who they are, what they specialize in and so forth.

The following are but a few suggested questions which you can expand on:

1. How long have you been practicing law in the court where my case will be filed?

2. What percentage of your practice is devoted to divorce work?

3. How many divorce cases are you presently handling? You're not asking for client names, just an estimate of the lawyer's current workload. One of the most common complaints, once a lawyer is hired, is that "They never seem to have enough time for me or my case." Busy is good, of course. It suggests the attorney is well regarded, but a lawyer who takes on too many cases cannot possibly be effective for you.
4. How many divorce cases have you tried to conclusion? This is important. If everything goes to pieces and you end up in court, you do not want to be the barber's first haircut. Or second. Or even third. There are a lot of attorneys out there who are terrific in a settlement negotiation or mediation, but they simply do not know their way around the courtroom.
5. How often do you engage in mediation?
6. What are the names of the best mediators you have used?
7. Please describe the path my case will take, and the timing involved. In response, expect to hear about the filing of your action, exchanging financial affidavits, sitting for depositions and so forth. As this is explained, be sure to ask follow-up questions so you know EXACTLY WHAT IS INVOLVED and HOW LONG THE LAWYER THINKS ALL THAT WILL TAKE. An experienced matrimonial attorney will know, so if you get a lot of vague hemming and hawing get the hell out of there pronto.
8. How much will all of this cost? You don't just want the total, mind you. You want a breakdown of all the various phases. What if we negotiate a settlement? Use a mediator? Have to go to trial? Each of these results will have a different price tag and you want the estimates for each.

We want to share a few more tips to aid you in this selection process:

Make sure your lawyer has a sense of empathy for your case. It has been said that it does not matter how nasty or disinterested a surgeon is. The only thing that counts is whether they have the skills to perform the operation. I do not disagree, but I have trouble analogizing the relationship between a doctor and patient with a lawyer and client. When you undergo surgery, you are almost always unconscious. Your personality traits, financial situation and profession do not matter at all to the physician. If he or she is there to remove a tumor, repair a muscle tear or perform a heart transplant, the only thing they will care about is your medical condition.

In a divorce, there will inevitably be times when you will be working side-by-side with your counsel. In a settlement conference, a mediation or a trial, the way you interact may be critical to the result achieved. If you are not impressed with the empathy, caring, and interest you experience in that first interview, I can assure you that things will not get better. In that initial meeting they are engaging in a sales pitch, do not forget that. They want you to hire them or they wouldn't be seeing you. If they do not dazzle you with their compassion and attention from the outset, move on.

NEVER stop asking questions of your attorney. And we mean NEVER. Too many people hire a lawyer and expect them to carry the ball across the finish line for them with little or no involvement from you. That is utter nonsense. You will have to be providing financial data, documents, and personal information all along the way. As you do, ask what it all means. Ask when you will be getting the same data from the other side. Ask about timing, about the progress of the case, anything at all that comes to mind. This is one time when curiosity is your ally.

Challenge your lawyer—if they are any good at what they do they will not mind and they will have the answers. If they do mind, then it is time for you to think about another attorney.

That leads to the next thought. We are not in favor of changing counsel in the middle of a case, but you also have to know that sometimes there is no choice. This is a simple concept—if you are not getting what you want from your lawyer it may be time to move on.

There is an important caveat here. Your lawyer is not a miracle worker. The fact you are not getting everything you want may not be their fault. Perhaps your expectations are unreasonable, and that is something the two of you should discuss. What I'm talking about here is an attorney who has become unresponsive, uninterested, or downright lazy. In that case, do not feel you are stuck with your initial choice. Remember, as we have said before, you are the boss and the lawyer works for you!

Here are some additional guidelines for selecting your lawyer:

Do you feel comfortable sharing personal details of your marriage?

Does the attorney seem truly interested in you and solving your problems?

Does the lawyer have associates, and how much of the work will be given to them? If there seems to be a lot of that involvement, ask to meet the associates as well.

Ask for a detailed list of action steps. In other words, what actions will they take, in what order, and what is the projected timeline?

You can go online to find out if the lawyer you are interviewing has had any disciplinary actions or complaints filed with the local bar association.

Comrades in arms

At best, divorce is a confrontational dynamic. We hope that yours is less contentious than many others, but even if you work everything out between the two of you, in the end you will still need an attorney. Whether your split turns into a Battle Royale or is a polite negotiation or mediation, it is critical that you see your counsel as someone who will have your best interests at heart and will fight for you when necessary.

This all may seem obvious, but it should never be forgotten. From the outset of the relationship with your lawyer it is important that you actually like the person. You do not have to become friends, nor do we even suggest that a social relationship is helpful to the process.

Nevertheless, you should not be represented by someone about whom you feel even a measure of antipathy toward their style or character. You will be comrades in arms in one of the most meaningful passages of your life. You will need to respect your advocate. You will need to rely on him/her doing everything they need to do in your best interests. You will need to be comfortable in asking questions, having conversations, and even challenging some of his/her decisions or advice.

There was a woman who chose her lawyer based on his reputation for being tough, ruthless, and sometimes nasty. Unfortunately, he did not leave those traits in the courthouse. Those features defined him as a person, leaving his client intimidated, fearful of disagreeing with advice he provided, and unable to express her true feelings. How do you think their interactions worked out for her?

Your attorney should be tough. You want someone who will do battle for you as they attempt to achieve a result you find acceptable if not downright positive. But those aggressive tendencies should not be practiced on you. Would you continue to use a physician who refused to fully discuss your condition or give advice you thought was beneficial to your health? Of course not. As brilliant as your doctor may be, you also want compassion, understanding and an ability to communicate with you in a meaningful and productive manner.

We have heard people say that if they did not "hit it off" in the first interview with their potential counsel, they knew they were in the wrong place. They were right. After all, if you do not get along with someone during a period of courtship what is that relationship going to look like when the going actually gets rough?

<u>Post-Divorce Issues</u>

There is no denying that many people end up in court, or at least in negotiations and arguments, even after the divorce is done. Circumstances change, financial issues arise, disputes over children surface, and so on. For many, these post-divorce skirmishes can be even more upsetting and expensive than the split itself.

Our first bit of advice here is obvious—avoid this syndrome like the plague. No matter how bitter the breakup was, try to resolve things like adults, without getting counsel and courts involved.

However, if this approach does not work—and sometimes it does not because one or the other party is still angry, or unreasonable, or whatever—you may need further legal representation. We mention this because, when your divorce is finalized, it is important that you not burn any bridges with your attorney. You may need him/her again, and they already know your entire case. Unless you feel your matter was poorly handled, you do not want to have to pay some new attorney to review your entire file—which any good lawyer will insist on doing— before moving ahead.

Therefore, in those early interviews when you are selecting someone to carry your banner into battle, be sure they will be willing to stay with you after the divorce is done, just in case problems arise. You want someone with the integrity to uphold what they had previously done for you and to remain responsible!

CHAPTER 6
SELECTING A THERAPIST

"There are many ways of getting strong, sometimes talking is the best way." Andre Agassi

Hopefully you do not take medication without the advice of a doctor or buy stock without speaking with your broker or—God forbid—try to play golf without a pro telling you how to swing a club.

Be honest with yourself. Even if you have been divorced before, you will still need help this time around. In fact, if you have been divorced before you also have things to learn about making a marriage work, right? This book is intended to help you, since there is nothing like having the voice of experience to guide you along the way, and the more personal that advice the better.

That brings us to the advisability of engaging the assistance of a qualified therapist, and just as we said, that lists of the best attorneys make us laugh, so do lists of the best therapists. Inclusion in those compilations usually represent a commercialization of the profession and may even involve payment by the mental health provider. We will discuss how we think you can choose wisely.

However, the first question we should ask is whether a counselor or therapist is a good idea for you. As has been said many times in this book, you may be struggling with a host of emotional reactions typically encountered in the divorce process. But you may not. Perhaps you are completing our questionnaires, having an honest look at yourself, your spouse, and your situation, and are dealing with all of the attendant issues. If so, we applaud you and encourage you to move on with your journey.

But if you are having difficulty, to the point where you think it would be valuable to get some help, then speaking with a therapist or counselor could be very useful. If that is where you are, we should have a look at some of the things you may be thinking or feeling. For the sake of simplicity, throughout this discussion the term counseling will be used to cover psychotherapy and all forms of counseling/therapy.

6.1 Another checklist

The following is a worksheet to help you decide if counseling is advisable. "Oh no!" you say. "Not another questionnaire!" Yes, but this is an easy one, and should also provide further insight into your situation.

Check all of the following statements you feel apply to you:

My marriage had me stuck in a place I did not want to be.

Many aspects of my marriage had me feeling upset and basically unable to relax. I find that I constantly think about what went wrong in my marriage.

My daily interactions with my spouse had me believing I am too sensitive. My marriage often made me depressed and sometimes I just felt like crying.

There was so much tension in the marriage, I began drinking too much alcohol. There was so much tension in the marriage, I began using drugs/narcotics.

I no longer read as much as I used to because I have difficulty concentrating. I do not feel as physically well as I used to.

I often feel afraid. I feel miserable.

I am haunted by the thought that I should have known not to marry this person. I have developed abnormal eating patterns.

I experience extreme mood swings. I feel hopeless.

I have panic attacks.

I believe my marriage was on a downhill track for many years. I know I feel anxious most of the time.

Checking even a few of the above statements would suggest that you could benefit from visiting a counselor. Naturally, if you checked more than a few categories, it only increases the likelihood that counseling will be valuable.

There are many different types of counseling. Most people going through a divorce want to gain a better understanding of what happened in the marriage. Some ask for help with parenting issues. Some want to take a look into their own personality issues. Others want to discuss what is next for them. Whatever your motivation, counseling can address your needs.

6.2 Why can't I just take a pill?

The intense stress of a divorce causes many people to consider the use of medication to lessen the feeling of anxiety and depression. While we want to be cautious about leaning on pharmaceuticals, it would be unfair to suggest that medication is never helpful. There are many number of psychological conditions where prescriptive help could be beneficial. These include chronic anxiety, depression, serious mood fluctuations, obsessive/compulsive behaviors, extreme withdrawal, or panic attacks, just to name a few common issues. If you have suffered from any of these, particularly if they began prior to the divorce decision, medication may be indicated.

Please remember, though, that for the overwhelming majority of people going through divorce, this is not the case. The emotional turmoil resulting from divorce is part of the normal rite of passage, as we have described earlier. Do not allow drugs—or alcohol for that matter—to become a dangerous crutch. Do not use the hiring of a therapist as a path to medications you do not need.

Counseling should help you cope with the various emotional upsets that may plague you and will provide benefits that last longer than medication without the underlying dangers of negative side effects. Counseling will teach you to address the feeling themselves and will furnish techniques to reduce the symptoms. These skills will not only offer methods you will utilize through the divorce, but in going forward into your happy future. You will probably find that the coping skills you learn are applicable to many aspects of your life, in addition to the issues produced by the divorce, and will last a lifetime.

It is axiomatic to say it is counter-productive to tell a person they must get into counseling. First, no one likes to be told they must do something. Second, counseling will not work unless you are committed to the process. But experience tells us it is important for you to consider the emotional load you are living with and to make the very personal decision if counseling will be a good move for you.

6.3 What sort of therapist should I see?

If you have decided to seek counseling, there are several professional fields from which to choose.

To become a psychiatrist a person must graduate from college, attend medical school and then complete a year of training in a hospital designed to treat patients with various types of mental health conditions. Many psychiatrists focus on the use of medication for intervention in psychological issues.

A clinical psychologist studies the brain, child and general development, the formation and function of emotions, and family processes. Psychologists must have a college education, a master's degree in psychology and go on for further study toward a Ph.D. or Psy.D. These two degrees should be considered equivalent. Some psychologists have attained a Diplomate status, which is the highest level of recognition and accreditation given by the American Psychological Association. The Diplomate (ABPP) is awarded after seven years of post-doctoral training, written and oral examination as well as an original research or treatment process presented to an examining committee of other Diplomates. You will recognize this status for a psychologist by seeing after his/her title, the letters ABPP.

Both the psychiatrist and clinical psychologist must be licensed in the state of their practice.

You may also encounter Licensed Clinical Social Workers (LCSW), who perform a variety of mental health therapies, but have different backgrounds and training than the psychologist and psychiatrist. The degree of LCSW usually requires a master's degree in Social Work. The LCSW is a licensed practitioner who is trained in the mental health branch of social work. The LCSW tends to consider not only a client's inventory of strengths and perceived weaknesses, but also the client's environment in their personal and professional life. There are many competent LCSW's who are in private practice, working with clients with all sorts of emotional interferences in their life.

You may also come across "mental health counselors" who help people manage and overcome mental and emotional disorders and problems with family and other relationships. Some states offer licensure to mental health counselors. They may have one of the following titles: Licensed Mental Health Counselor (LMHC), Licensed Professional Counselor (LPC) or Licensed Clinical Professional Counselor (LCPC). For any of these categories, the individual has earned a master's degree in a relevant psychological field, completed a specific number of training hours, under supervision, and passed a licensing exam in their state.

You can choose from any of these categories. In most instances, psychiatrists will be the most expensive, accredited psychologists the next costliest, while social workers and mental health counselors less so.

6.4 Finding the right therapist

In selecting a therapist, the two most important elements are:

1. Whether the two of you have a good rapport, preferably right from the start; and
2. You have selected a professional, trained to help you through the various struggles inherent in divorce.

Be sure to find out what he or she is known for, and what they may specialize in. You are going through a divorce. If a particular psychiatrist is renowned for work with schizophrenics, he/she may be a bad choice. Likewise, a psychologist who is highly regarded for work with addictive personalities may be cause to look elsewhere. This is all just common sense. You want someone you can easily relate to, who has helped a lot of people on the road to Splitsville. In order to assist in the process, a few thoughts:

Experience matters. One of the main reasons for seeing a therapist, rather than simply talking to a friend, is experience. As already outlined, look for a therapist who is experienced in treating the problems that you have.

Learn about different treatment orientations. Many therapists practice a blend of orientations and approaches. Ask about their treatment types and styles. We had a client who spent three sessions with a counselor, pouring out her heart. When she finally asked for some advice, the counselor said, "Oh, you want answers. I'm not in the answer business, I am in the listening business." Three hours wasted!

Check licensing. Credentials are not everything, but make sure the therapist holds a current license and is in good standing with the state regulatory board. Regulatory boards vary by state and profession. You may also want to check for complaints against the therapist.

Trust your gut. Even if your therapist looks great on paper, if the connection does not feel right from the start—if you do not trust the person or feel like they truly care—go with another choice.

But counseling is expensive. This can be true, and concern about costs is not unusual, but we offer a few common-sense tips. Be sure to explore your insurance. Many people do not realize that they may have some coverage, especially for "in network providers." See what sort of help is offered in your community, at the local hospital, health service agencies and so forth. You may also find that the professional you seek will consider a reduced fee arrangement.

The cost of counseling may seem like a significant expense, but the benefits can be well worth it.

Remember, you deserve the support! Whatever choice you make, look to counseling as a means to help you cope with a wide range of issues. Anyone can enjoy the benefits of therapy, whether you want to work through the end of your marriage, set new life goals or establish healthy relationships. You do not need to be in a debilitating crisis to get

support. You deserve whatever help you can get. Being proactive about your mental health should also prevent your concerns from festering into larger problems. Counseling can bring a relief from symptoms and restore your quality of life. You have undertaken a difficult journey, from a failed marriage to a divorce, and you deserve some relief. Enjoy the time speaking about yourself with someone trained to listen and to provide guidance.

6.5 A list of some of the benefits you can expect to get from counselling:

You will be happy to know that this is a list you need do nothing about except to read and consider it:

A counselor will help you to define realistic goals and to develop strategies to achieve those goals. A counselor will not tell you what to do, but should provide recommendations for how you can act on your own to get where you want to be.

Counseling will help you to learn more about yourself.

Whether you are single or have already found a new relationship, counseling will help you to address difficulties with relating to others and enable you to have more fulfilling relationships—and hopefully not repeat mistakes from your past.

Divorce can often damage self-confidence and self-esteem. Counseling will help you to develop a better sense of self-worth and recover your mojo.

Having a confidential confidant, with whom you can share the multitude of emotions created by divorce, will help you cope better with all aspects of life and to feel better about your decision and yourself. There is tremendous value in having a safe and private person to talk with about many of the very sensitive issues that went into the marriage relationship and the decision for divorce.

Divorce can bring on anxiety and depression, and counseling will help you better understand the origin of those feelings and how to eliminate them.

If you are dealing with issues of self-medication to squash the troubling emotions and behavior, counseling can help you control the use of alcohol or other substances.

Counseling will promote the development of new healthy behaviors and habits which will move you toward more satisfying relationships in all areas of your life.

Many people in the divorce situation suffer from lack of sleep, poor nutrition, or a withdrawal from physical exercise. Counseling will enable you to combat those issues.

Most people in counseling feel that they come away with a much better understanding of what led to their unhappy marriage and the multitude of feelings that caused the divorce decision.

6.6 A Post Script: Beware of helpful friends

Marriages are like fingerprints, everyone is unique. Listening to your friends' opinions about your divorce, the inner workings of your relationship, or your financial circumstances is as useless as having them analyze your personality. There are experts for these things, and that is who you should turn to for answers. It is wonderful to have the support and empathy of those around you, and they are undoubtedly well-meaning, but do not mistake that for worthwhile advice. Having your friends play amateur therapist—or lawyer—is not a great idea!

You probably have friends who have been divorced, but that does not make them experts on the subject. In fact, their opinions will be influenced by their own facts and circumstances, which are inevitably different than yours. And remember, they will not have to live with the decisions you finally make, but you will. No matter how close the person is to you, no matter how well meaning, they can never really know the totality of what you are experiencing or feel.

It is understandable that you will want support and compassion from your friends and relatives. That is a healthy instinct. You will want them to listen to your plight, to agree that you are right, that your spouse is wrong, and to offer unconditional warmth, if not love. But that sort of empathy is not the same thing as advice, which will always be tainted by their own experiences, not to mention their lack of expertise.

If you listen to the average cocktail chatter, you know that everyone has an opinion on just about everything. Over the years you have been bombarded by so much personal propaganda and media input that sometimes it becomes difficult to sort out your own beliefs. Asking for advice is natural, because you believe those closest to you have your best interests at heart. Just remember, please, that it is not the road to Splitsville that is paved with good intentions.

Trust yourself. You know what you feel. You know what went wrong in your marriage. You know what you need to move on and find happiness. Do not confuse support with advice, and never substitute another person's judgment for what you know in your heart to be true.

Whatever feels right for you on this journey will take you to where you should be.

CHAPTER 7
TIME TO DISCUSS LOVE AND SEX

You really have come quite a distance since we began this trek.

First, you were brave enough to identify the issues that led to the end of your marriage, some of which may have even been your own mistakes. You confronted all of that—your spouse's shortcomings as well as your own—so you will hopefully never make any of those missteps again.

Then you had the integrity to look at the issues you had to face along this path, to face down those demons and then consider techniques to help you get past them.

Finally, you rolled up your sleeves and got down to the action steps required to get your divorce. Compiling financial data, bank and credit card statements, and completing a financial affidavit that is a pain in the neck for everyone. You either chose, or are in the process of choosing, the method to wrap up the divorce; the lawyer who can best serve you; and maybe a therapist to accompany you on that part of the journey.

We thought it was high time, then, to have a look at two subjects that factor prominently in every marriage and divorce, to one extent or another—love and sex.

Unless your marriage was the result of some medieval political arrangement, it is likely that love had something to do with how the two of you got together. We, therefore, pose a basic question—what did love mean to you back then? This becomes significant because a deterioration of what you once felt is integral to the breakup of the marriage. As you evaluate what part love played in your marital choice and your decision to divorce—

not to mention how it will impact your future intimate relationships—you should want to know how you defined love then, and how you define it now.

A corollary to that is a second inquiry—what was your attitude toward sex back then, what did it become during the marriage, and what is it now?

As to both of these subjects, it is highly improbable that your views, definitions and attitudes have not changed. This becomes important as you move ahead in search of a new relationship, a sense of fulfillment, and happiness.

7.1 Let's talk about love.

Generally speaking, *loving* someone means a deep commitment and an intimate connection to that person. It is not merely *liking* someone, which consists primarily of having positive feelings towards that person and finding their company rewarding and pleasant. Research supports the notion that we can experience warmth and deep feelings of closeness towards people we *like* and, in some situations, we may even choose to become intimate with them—but that is not *love.*

Most of the time, loving someone includes all of the feelings that go into liking a person, but ironically that is not always true. You have probably known people who love someone without liking them all that much, since love exists on a far more emotional plane. In fact, some marriages fail when the parties come to dislike each other so much they cannot bear to continue the relationship, even though some measure of love endures. Most psychologists find that a true feeling of love has the following three components:

- **Intimacy**, which means there are deep feelings of closeness, connectedness, and bondedness.
- **Passion**, which traditionally involves feelings and desires that lead to physical attraction, romance, and sexual consummation.

- **Commitment**, which involves feelings that lead a person to remain with someone and move toward shared goals.

Romantic love typically includes two sub-categories of love: *passionate love* and *companionate love*. Passionate love is when you say you feel you are "*in love*"—accompanied by feelings of physical attraction, the need to be with that other individual, the sense of emptiness when you are apart and all those little tells such as a quickening pulse or the tendency to find yourself thinking about the other person when you are apart. *Companionate love* is not felt as intensely, but is important to the connection since it includes a desire for emotional intimacy and commitment. Always remember, however, these factors are very personal, vary greatly, and you should never compare yourself to any objective standard, real or imagined, nor to anyone else you know. The key is to understand what is important to you, what you value and how those things cause you to interact with a partner.

As you have worked through our various questions, hopefully you are coming to an honest understanding of what you felt when your marriage began, how that developed, deteriorated and then ended. It is sad to review all of the negatives involved, but it will assist you in shaking off the lingering pain and aid you in creating a new life, since you now have the ability to consider what has become important to you as you move forward. For instance, is passion as important as trust? Is a sexual attraction as important as a feeling of companionship?

The following is a True-False questionnaire developed by researchers* that will give you an objective way of evaluating how love evolved throughout the marriage. This is another easy worksheet:

1. My spouse often talked about planning future activities together, planning for us in a way that demonstrated regard for us as a couple.
2. Despite our problems, my spouse treated me with respect.
3. My spouse wants to spend their free time with me.

4. My spouse frequently told other people positive things about me.
5. My spouse touched me a lot, in both comforting and sexual ways.
6. My spouse listened to me when we were talking.
7. My spouse confided in me.
8. My spouse treated me as a priority.
9. My spouse always looked out for my good, and I felt protected.
10. Whatever our differences, I always knew my spouse loved me.
11. My spouse made frequent expressions of love toward me.

As you will realize, often an answer of TRUE or FALSE to these statements cannot be given. These elements of your relationship inevitably changed during the marriage, so part of the exercise is to assist you in identifying what aspects of love are most important to you. The idea was not to trick you, but to provoke thought that will lead you to insights about your attitude toward love—past, present, and future.

7.2 What about sex?

As we all know, sex is an important component of any romantic relationship. Whatever your sexual needs and appetites, and those of your former partner, our guess is that physical intimacy had something to do with your mutual attraction, certainly in the early days. Sex also offers a lot of benefits outside of pleasure. Studies have shown that a healthy sexual relationship will improve self-confidence, provide a better connection with your own body and help you bond with your partner in a positive manner of expressing love and caring. Anyone who has engaged in satisfying sexual activity will certainly agree it is also an excellent stress reliever.

As obvious as some of these observations may be, there are things we need to point out as a preface to our discussion of sex:

1. People have different sex drives. Simply stated, some of us need or want sex more or less often than others.
2. Under the basic laws of attraction, the more our sexual needs and desires match those of our partner, the better our sex life—and relationship—is likely to be. Obviously, the opposite is also true.
3. Your sex drive is likely to change over time, and so will your partner's. One of you may want to engage in physical intimacy less frequently, or more often. Add to that the probability that your respective interest in different types of sex will expand or narrow. Rarely do the years go by without some sort of changes.
4. Sex means different things to different people. For some, kissing and holding each other, then finishing with intercourse in the missionary position, is satisfying. Others enjoy receiving or giving oral sex. Some like to experiment with different positions, bondage, vibrators, and other sex toys, spanking, risking sex in public, and so on. Once again, the more your cravings and tastes are in synch with your partner's, the more fulfilled the two of you are likely to feel.
5. Your physical health and condition, and that of your partner, will affect your sexual attraction and compatibility.
6. The ability you and your partner have to discuss your respective sexual needs and taboos will have a tremendous effect on how the two of you relate sexually, and otherwise.

This section, which focuses on the role of sex in marriage and your decision to divorce, is included not just to help you in the future, but also because it is a frequent topic of concern for many of the people we counsel. One of the questions often asked is, "Is sex essential for a good marriage?"

Sex is not everything in a good marriage but, for many people, a healthy, regular sex life matters quite a bit. Sexual intimacy increases emotional closeness in marriage, this is obvious. The affection, understanding, warmth, and compassion shared between a couple are also expressions of their bond, as physical and emotional intimacy build on each other.

Another reason sex is important in a marriage is that it tends to build trust. A successful sexual relationship requires vulnerability. By its very nature, having sex of any type involves you and your spouse literally "baring it all" to each other. In so doing, you open yourselves up to the possibility of either an experience of acceptance or rejection from each other at a basic psychological and physical level. We have mentioned many times in this book how important trust is to a happy marriage, and when your sexual connection is strengthened the marriage relationship grows stronger.

Thousands of studies have also proved that an active sexual life has demonstrable health benefits. It is good for the body and the mind, can boost your immune system, alleviate stress, improve heart health, and new studies are even showing that it benefits your memory.

Then there is the basic truth, that love and sex are intertwined. Could you have fallen for someone you did not enjoy kissing? Someone for whom you did not feel some sort of physical attraction? Someone who did not set your heart beating faster at the prospect of seeing them, holding them or making love with them?

If we can fairly assume you felt some or all of those things at some point, you have to ask yourself, WHAT HAPPENED?

As suggested above and elsewhere in this book, it is more than likely that one or both of you changed. Sexual needs that might have been in synch at one time diverged. One of you wanted to experiment, while the other refused, or became even more conservative. One or both of you felt the desire to meet your needs outside the marriage. One of you no longer felt sex was as important as you once did.

Whatever your personal circumstances, we feel certain that you now have the skills and insight to answer this all-important question for yourself. Just be honest about what happened, without ascribing blame, without judging. If you can do that, you will continue on the path to freeing yourself from the upset that occurred and preparing for a healthier relationship in the future.

If you have any doubts about that, go back and read points 1 through 6, above. Make a brutally honest appraisal of where you were and are in each of those categories. Then decide what you want for your future, while reminding yourself that you are only human and that you will continue to evolve, change, and grow.

Putting aside, for a moment, the clinical appraisals and advice we have been providing, let us remember that SEX SHOULD BE FUN! If, during your marriage, sex made you feel abused, put upon, put down, disrespected, unappreciated, inadequate, unsatisfied, embarrassed, or otherwise unhappy, then be very glad you have traveled to Splitsville.

Given the importance this issue has for so many people we have counseled, we thought we should briefly examine some reasons, and examples, of why sex becomes such a large factor in marriage, in the hope that this will provide insight as you move into your next relationship. Some of these examples are graphic, but we feel they are valuable:

Discrepancy in sexual desire

As already pointed out, it is not uncommon for one partner in a marriage to desire sex more than the other, a difference that may become worse over time. This is an obvious problem, since one spouse may feel inadequate and pressured while the other feels dissatisfied and a sense of rejection. This discrepancy in desire can put the marriage at risk depending on how wide the divide becomes.

How things can change over time

Cindy

Cindy was an attractive 35-year-old woman who had been married for ten years. She described her pre-marital sexual relationship as nothing less than torrid, when she and her fiancé were having sex four or five times per week, sometimes more than once a night. Over time, however, despite her husband's expectation that they should engage in some form of sexual activity with the same frequency, her interest had waned. She felt guilty, particularly because she could not attribute her lack of desire to any of his behaviors or attitudes. She was simply not interested.

Cindy admitted that she was bewildered by the decline in her sexual appetite and admitted that it was damaging their marriage. At this point, she suspected that her husband had found another woman, which he denied, but she felt sure he was only seeing this other woman for the sex.

Cindy had thought a great deal about the change she had experienced since they were married. She claimed to have read just about everything that has been written on the subject and was finally coming to terms with a key concern—that she had never had a real orgasm, not even when she and her husband were active in their pre-marital phase.

She consulted with her physician, who suggested that she try to relax during sex, to avoid putting pressure on herself, but that did not help. Cindy felt guilty since she had been faking it since she and Carl began going together, although she insisted that he never knew. She was actually proud of the way she could feign a climax, with moaning, arching of her back, heavy breathing and all of that. But she also admitted that, once they were married, she abandoned the act. Instead, she tried to talk to Carl about her lack of interest, but he was unwilling to engage in that conversation, perhaps unable to deal with her decreasing sexual attraction to him.

Left to explore the problem on her own, she explained that she worked at a very demanding, fatiguing job; that she was deeply stressed by certain financial problems at home; and that she received no help from Carl with cooking, cleaning, or other household chores. Her recent suspicion that he was having an affair was extremely painful, particularly since the time for her to have children was growing short. Worst of all, Carl was unwilling to engage in joint counseling or even support her in seeking counseling for herself.

He ultimately concluded that the best thing was for them to divorce and for her to find a relationship that was more in sync with her needs.

Cindy's story is certainly not unique. The difference in desire for sex is one of the most frequent issues married couples experience. In Cindy's case, her partner was unwilling to address the issue and, when your partner does not have the skills or interest in examining the problem, it will never be resolved.

Alice

Alice presented a different set of issues that accounted for her diminished sexual interest—she was a victim of childhood abuse.

Beginning as a young girl, and into her teenage years, her stepfather would sometimes come into her bedroom, force her legs open and massage her until she had what he regarded as an orgasm. Sometimes that would be followed by forcing her to perform oral sex on him.

When she began dating John, Alice felt she would be able to overcome this history, but she now admitted she could never get those awful pictures out of her mind, especially after she married. John began to remind her of her stepfather in appearance and even in the kind of things he would say to her in bed. She knew he was trying to be affectionate and even seductive when he whispered beautiful things about her breasts, her thighs, and her vagina, but these were too similar to the things her stepfather would say as he molested her.

Just as Alice was incapable of telling her mother what was happening when she was a child, she felt incapable of sharing any of those experiences with John. As a result, she did not explain her reactions to the things he would say to her. It finally became obvious to her that it was not only the abuse, but also the secret she was keeping, that got in the way of her having a gratifying sexual relationship with John. Fortunately for Alice, she was finally willing to address all of this in therapy and John had the sensitivity and empathy to help her confront these demons.

It is not uncommon for abuse in childhood to emerge as a significant interference in the sexual relationship someone experiences in marriage. It is understandable how it can create a discrepancy in sexual desire and some negative feelings about sex. Alice and John were among the lucky ones, who found a way to work it out.

Motherhood made me do it!

Vanessa was beautiful, shapely and, by any objective standard, a sexy woman. She married Greg, a handsome man, and they began their intimate relationship like a car that begins running in fourth gear. There was no stopping them.

They socialized, traveled, doted on each other, and made love like two teenagers in heat—albeit with the benefit of being two fully experienced adults. Nothing was off-limits, nothing too kinky for them to try—vibrators, satin ropes, spankings, blindfolds, dressing up in erotic outfits, making love in every room of their home, in every imaginable position. They might suddenly engage in oral sex on a quiet Saturday afternoon, anal sex in the middle of the night, warm oil massages that would bring them both to climax.

Then they had a daughter and, a little more than a year after that, they had a son. And everything changed.

Vanessa suffered from post-partum depression. She had difficulty coping with the needs of two small children. She became terrified that she would never regain her wonderful physique. She feared that she looked older and haggard from the loss of sleep occasioned by the demands of two infants, Vanessa became a supermom, dedicating herself almost exclusively to her two children and almost entirely ignoring her role as a wife. Then she became overcome with guilt, that she was thinking of herself and her children to the exclusion of her relationship with Greg, and ultimately lost all interest in sex.

That result was owed to many things, including her fear of having another child, which should have been easily addressed. The larger issue, however, was the impact on her sense of self. Before they had children, she and Greg were insatiable sexual partners. Now she viewed that behavior as inappropriate. She could not be a mother and a slut, as she now viewed her prior role. The fire was out and she had neither the desire nor the interest to rekindle that flame with her husband.

As you could easily predict, things between Vanessa and her husband went from bad to worse and, after a few painful years she wanted a divorce. Greg had cheated on her repeatedly, and she could not understand why his needs went on unabated while she had frozen up. He begged her to see a therapist, but she refused, convinced that she was now who she needed to be, an overly attentive helicopter mom who had no time or energy for the man with whom she had shared such intimacy and love.

It was one of the saddest possible divorces, because there were so many positives that could have been recovered. She came to regret what happened, especially just a few years later, when her children's need for her overbearing place in their lives became less and less. But at the time, she could not see the bleak future she was creating for herself.

It was an ironic twist of fate, where the love between two people created beautiful children, but Vanessa's view of motherhood destroyed the relationship. She simply could not make the necessary adjustments, even for some reasonable period of time, so that she and Greg might recapture what they had.

As it turned out, her lack of self-awareness led to another marriage which also ended in divorce, leaving her sad, empty, and alone.

We do not suggest this syndrome is the sole purview of the wife. An obvious corollary to this dilemma is when one of the partners becomes so immersed in work that there is neither time nor energy for sex and romance.

As you move ahead on the path to happiness, always remember— love, sex, intimacy and caring all take time and effort, and are all worth the rewards.

<u>What happened to our physical attraction?</u>

The loss of physical attraction between marriage partners often occurs as time goes by. That diminished sense of desire can contribute to a decision to divorce. Remember, if it has been part of what happened in your marriage, and a big part of the reason for divorce, you are not unique or alone.

<u>When the magic just disappears</u>

Unlike Vanessa and Greg, Franny and Hans shared a more measured personal life.

Sexual intimacy was important, but it was not the centerpiece of their relationship. According to Franny, they would make love in what she called "traditional positions." There were no whips and chains or battery-operated devices in use, and these encounters were regular but not frequent. Once every week or two seemed natural to both of them, and both of them seemed satisfied—until those weeks became months.

The difficult part for Franny was not the lack of sexual intercourse. As already suggested, she was not especially passionate. But she missed the touching, fondling, and holding those expressions of love and warmth that were so important to her, a validation of their love for each other. She claimed that when she tried to discuss the situation, Hans would back away, literally, and figuratively. He did not want to address any of that, until one day he said something she was left to relive over and over.

We are going to stop here to make a point that is critical to a full comprehension of the interactions between people, whether they are friends, lovers, or parents and children. WORDS CAN WOUND MORE DEEPLY THAN A KNIFE. Just speak with a woman who has been physically abused and you will learn this basic truth—that the dreadful, insulting words hurled at her during these assaults did far more lasting damage than any of the slaps or punches inflicted on her. The pain that does not go away comes from those awful things that were said, horrible sentiments that—once uttered—can never be taken back again.

So, it was for Franny. When she finally pushed Hans, imploring him to understand what had happened, he told her that the magic between them had simply disappeared. Which was hurtful enough. But when she asked for an explanation of what that meant to him what he thought had happened, he said, "I can't stand the way you smell."

Admittedly, there are many number of possible reactions to that statement. One might force a laugh or ask Hans if she should try a different perfume or change her deodorant or soap. But having said it, he made things worse, detailing how her feminine aromas now turned him off; how her basic body odor had become an issue; how even her breath was offensive.

What was she to do with that indictment of her personal being? How could she ever see building a bridge back to what they had been?

Franny was inconsolable. She offered to see a doctor to handle what had become an issue for Hans, but he was convinced it would do no good. She suggested they see a marriage counsellor, but he quite literally scoffed at the idea. What is a psychotherapist going to do about a problem like this? She asked if this was all some sort of ruse, a cover-up for the fact that he was seeing someone else, but he flatly denied it, and she found no evidence of his having an affair.

As you would expect, Franny's self-confidence was irredeemably shaken. She saw a therapist on her own, who suggested an obvious explanation—perhaps Hans had lost his own sex drive and had to find some way to blame her, rather than confront his own growing impotence. Whatever the reason for this drastic turn, their relationship was done.

Their divorce became inevitable, and it took years before she was comfortable sleeping with another man. Yet slowly she rose from the depths of self-doubt and created a new relationship for herself, which was not easy, but it makes the lesson here clear.

Whatever might have happened to the sexual chemistry between you and your former partner, remember that you must never allow your partner's failures or criticisms to damage you. It took two of you to build that connection, and each of you had a share in how it ended.

If I can take care of myself, why can't you do the same?

Over time, Daphne found that she no longer felt physically attracted to Felix. A large part of that, in her view, was how her husband "let himself go." He became heavy and bloated looking. He never exercised, claiming he was too busy working to make time for all that "new age nonsense."

But Daphne worked hard to keep in shape, and regarded his attitude as wrong-headed, unhealthy and disrespectful of her—she was being taken for granted. It got to the point that she could not even imagine how she initially saw him as attractive and began to feel repulsed. She tried showing him photographs of how they looked when they were first married, pointing to how little she had changed and how much he had. But Felix insisted that people aged, and that was that.

If you went through anything like this, you will understand Daphne's frustration and upset. Losing her feelings of physical attraction toward Felix represented much more than just sex, it was all about fading intimacy and a lack of caring. Daphne began avoiding having to see him undress at night. She made sure that she did not touch him in bed, because she did not "want to give him any ideas," and she quickly turned away if he seemed to make sexual advances toward her. She described her reaction to "the wandering hand between her legs," causing her to move to the edge of the bed. Daphne found that this loss of physical attraction was not related to a decrease in her own sexual desire, because she missed having sex.

Many people who experience this loss of attraction consider it as the first sign of the romance fading. Often, the other spouse attributes it to a difference in sex drive between them. Whatever the source, the loss of sexual attraction is a real and a definite phenomenon. If you have done what you can to stay in shape, maintain a healthy weight, attend to personal grooming and even dressing in ways that will please your partner, you have every right to expect the same. If your spouse did not reciprocate, it was not only a lack of respect for them, but also revealed something about their attitude toward you.

Successful marriages are never perfect. Marriages succeed when the partners are able to face adversity, differences and upset, and work together to resolve these things. Your partner's lack of interest, rejection, and especially a refusal to address the problems, is never acceptable. If you feel any part of that was your fault—such as in the prior example—then as you move ahead, be sure you do all you can to be the best YOU possible. Then you will be able to find the person who appreciates that and loves you for it!

It is very hurtful to think you are not desired by a person you have loved. When your partner will not even deal with the issue, it could easily lead to the feeling that there is something missing in you, or that you have something wrong with you. Some people will gravitate to self-blame, but that is a destructive path. If there is no willingness by your partner to confront waning sexual activity and a lack of intimacy, your marriage will inevitably sink into a cycle of frustration, self-doubt, and unhappiness.

As mentioned above, be sure you are being honest with yourself. If you think you need to lose five or 10 pounds, then you should do it. If you need to undertake actions geared to self-improvement, then hurry up and start. This is your life, live it to the fullest and you will find no shortage of admirers.

Finding the "sex" that works for you

The word "sex" covers a lot of territory. Some people think of it as intercourse in the missionary position, as if that is the beginning and end of the subject. This, of course, is not true. As we mentioned at the beginning of this section, "sex" means different things to different people. Intercourse can be achieved in any number of positions. If you doubt this, check out the Kama Sutra or a book from a few decades ago, The Joy of Sex. There is rubbing, tickling, massaging and all sorts of tactile experiences, many of which can lead to orgasm. There is masturbation, mutual or otherwise. There is kissing, hugging and many varieties of affection that are themselves a subcategory of "sex." There is oral sex, both fellatio and cunnilingus. There is anal sex. Role playing. There are innumerable sex toys available, some driven by electricity others not. Some people enjoy giving or getting a spanking or engage in other forms of sado-masochism (safely, we urge).

The list does not end there, but we wanted to provide an overview since some of these activities are not interesting to some people and downright repugnant to others. The point for our discussion here is this—different strokes for different folks. It is obvious that the best sexual relationships are those where the partners are in sync about which options are the most pleasurable and which are non-starters. The key is for you to find what works for the two of you and not allow preconceived notions or societal taboos to interfere with a satisfying physical connection.

Do what pleases you and your partner. If sexual issues contributed to your marriage ending, be sure in your next relationship to find a partner who relates to how you feel about the myriad options. If someone finds oral sex "dirty" and you revel in receiving or giving it—or both—move on. If someone is into "domination," whips and chains, and you react best to tender displays of passion, then find another playmate. If you like to introduce mechanical devices in bed and your new mate thinks it too kinky, you may want to look elsewhere.

You get the idea.

Do not let physical issues impair sexual gratification.

In an age with so many pharmaceutical advancements, please do not let a physical problem interfere with your fun. Just a few thoughts on some of those difficulties you may have encountered:

Premature ejaculation

Bud and his wife had ceased to have any sexual contact because he suffered from premature ejaculation. His wife Sissy had become so frustrated that she would resort to all sorts of name-calling, mocked him for his physical infirmity and accused him of not caring about her pleasure—all of which obviously made things worse.

Bud began to think the issue was caused by his ambivalent feelings about his wife, and his fantasies of having intercourse with a "sexy blond." He did not look at the possible reasons for this fantasy and would not consult a physician or a sex therapist regarding his tendency to ejaculate within seconds of entering Sissy. After five years, Sissy said she had endured this long enough and that it was time for a divorce.

Bud continued to rationalize, believing it had to do with Sissy and his fantasies about sex with another woman. As the divorce progressed, he convinced himself that he was not attracted to his wife, that it was all her fault, and why he thought about other women when they were about to have intercourse.

After the divorce, he came to realize that the problem could not be Sissy, since it persisted. His sex life became almost nonexistent since he was too embarrassed to be with other women. He finally sought help, and soon determined that he was suffering from a nervous condition that related to incidents of masturbation when he was an adolescent. With the help of a good therapist and some medication he reclaimed his sexual life.

For her part, Sissy went for counseling to ensure that it was not anything about her that caused Bud's issue. Her self-esteem returned and she found a satisfying relationship with another man.

When your divorce is done and you are ready to get on with your life, be sure to address any sexual concerns you may have so that you never repeat mistakes from the past. We cannot urge this often enough.

Erectile dysfunction

For the last two years of their six-year marriage, Teddy had been unable to get an erection. Marie tried every technique she read about, but to no avail. Marie even engaged in a number of things she basically found unpleasant, but those did not resolve their problem. Marie felt a deep sense of hurt that he was unwilling to seek medical advice.

Marie believed that it is a physical problem. However, Teddy would not seek help, claiming that taking Viagra or any of the other similar medications were "strictly for wimps." She was left feeling unwanted, unloved and unwilling to live the rest of her life with this frustration.

Marie is a very attractive woman who believed that she had done all she could to either get Teddy excited or to get him to seek help. She decided that life was too short to spend in this situation, and finally filed for a divorce.

If you might solve a major problem by taking a pill, we urge you to consult with your doctor and determine all the available options.

Other medical issues

Lois stopped having intercourse with her husband because she found it too painful. She underwent several intense physical evaluations and was ultimately diagnosed with a congenital condition consisting of a narrowing of the vaginal canal. Surgery was an option, but she was fearful of surgery. As someone who believed that sex was all about the missionary position for intercourse, she was not interested in experimenting with other forms of sexual pleasure.

Her husband, Frank, was not happy with either of his wife's decisions. He could not tolerate her prosaic attitude about other forms of sexual pleasure since she refused to go through a fairly simple procedure that would alleviate the problem.

Lois felt his attitude—about a real physical issue interfering with sex—was a rejection of her and an expression of how little true feeling he has for her. She believed that having a legitimate physical limitation and her reluctance to engage in anything other than routine intercourse, left them in an impossible position, which could only be resolved by divorce. This decision was enforced by her suspicion that her husband was looking for other women to make up for the sex that was missing in their relationship.

There are certainly any number of physical and health related reasons that can interfere with sex in the marital relationship. However, as can be seen in the above examples, the attitude about the problem is at the core of the failure of the relationship. There are medications and procedures available today for many of these impediments, but both partners must be willing to explore the options and work together towards a resolution.

If this was an issue in your marriage, with either you or your spouse having the physical impairment, you can see how it is easy to blame that for the failure of the relationship. Much of the time, the true problem lies in the way the two partners react to the situation and interact with each other. Whatever the cause of the sexual impediment, it usually results in one or both of the couple feeling rejected and the consequential damage to self-esteem.

As you embark on this next phase of your life remember to keep an open mind with respect to how problems can be solved when there is empathy and love.

CHAPTER 8
TRY TO REMEMBER—YOUR CHILDREN DID NOT ASK FOR THIS

Your children did not destroy your marriage. On the road to Splitsville, never lose sight of that. They did not ask to have parents who discovered their relationship did not work out. They did not cause the dissension, bickering or bad behavior.

That said, we have already made the point that staying in a bad marriage for the good of your children is a mistake. It does not work for them, and it will not work for you. What you need to do on this journey is constantly assess how it is affecting them and to identify the adjustments you should be making for their benefit.

The more you fight during and after the divorce process, the more bitter things become, the worse it will be for your children, and you may be creating scars they will carry for life. You may also be doing permanent damage to your relationship with them.

Some parents report that they held a family type meeting and told their kids that mommy and daddy are splitting, but the reasons for the split have nothing to do with them. These parents say that they emphasize that they will always love each of their children and that everything will work out for them in the end.

But these are just words, and your children are not so easily fooled. They will not be persuaded by what you SAY, but by your ACTIONS.

8.1 Adult children of divorce

Loving parents worry about the effects of a divorce on their children. The predominant concern seems to occur when the children are in their preteen and teenage years. We acknowledge that this is a critical time for children to experience their parents' divorce, and we will discuss the issues they experience and suggest various ways to deal with that later in this chapter.

However, there is another group of children that deserve attention and understanding, the adult children of divorce. The number of those affected is growing, as the divorce rate among couples who have been married more than twenty years is increasing. Those adult children dealing with their parents' divorce is frequent enough that they have acquired an acronym, ACOD. Even though older children may have developed more coping mechanisms than adolescents, divorce will still have a powerful effect.

You might think adult children will find it easier to accept and understand their parents' decision to split, but it actually presents a unique series of questions and challenges. In our experience, the young child in a divorce can be viewed as an innocent bystander, with no responsibility for the situation they find themselves in. Adult children, on the other hand, often get dragged into becoming active participants in the situation. One of the most common ways this occurs is when one of the parents seeks emotional support, effectively asking their son or daughter to "take sides." Too often, there is little or no awareness or concern for the effect this will have.

Pick a side!

Peter first learned how bad things had become when his father came to him, asking Peter to speak with his mother about her asking for a divorce. Peter related his father's approach: "Pete, you know that we've had a happy family, but I think your mother has gone bonkers. She's not thinking straight, claiming we have a miserable marriage and wanting a divorce. Please, talk to her, I know you can straighten her out."

Peter said, "He's putting me in a terrible situation because we really didn't have a happy family. Mom was always taking care of us and he was never around. Sure, we had all the money we wanted and got whatever we asked for, but even when he was around, he spent no time with us. He occupied himself by working on his antique cars, never once coming to Jimmy's soccer games or Lizzie's dance recitals. Now I'm caught in the middle and my wife, Carole, thinks I have to tell him that I won't. So now Carole and I are having arguments about it. I really think I should talk to my mother, but Carole and I are going to have a baby in six months, and she doesn't want me mixed up in their divorce.

"My father's also gone to my sister Liz, asking her to do the same thing he's asking me. She's married with two children of her own, and she said no, even told him that she understands why mom wants a divorce. Liz admitted to me she has enough of her own feelings about the divorce and no energy to support him, especially since she understands mom wanting out. He wants us to be his confidante and to side with him, and she said we can't get in that role. She says we have no business intruding in their private world.

"Here I am at twenty-seven years old and I feel totally unequipped to handle this. If you asked me before, I would have said that it's much easier for an adult to handle their parents' divorce than a young child. I now see that may not be true because here I am an adult, married, and about to have my own child, and I feel totally unsure of what to do, and none of my friends have any advice on how I should handle it."

We should understand Peter's confusion as to how to act, given the bind he has been put in. This is not an uncommon situation, and you are cautioned about asking an adult child to take sides or to intervene in your divorce. It places an unfair burden on an adult child to ask for that kind of an intervention, especially if the child is being asked to convince the other parent that divorce is "wrong."

<u>The con man</u>

Beth was married to an accomplished con man. Let's call him Fred.

Fred was a respected businessman, loving husband, father, and even taught Sunday school at their church—but it was all a pile of fertilizer! He was a liar, a philanderer and, ultimately, a convicted criminal.

And my client never had a clue.

Say what you might, but Beth is a loving, trusting, intelligent woman who could not imagine who her husband really was. Not many people could. Fred fooled the entire community for many years, not to mention business associates and law enforcement. By the time his Ponzi scheme came crashing down there was nowhere for him to hide, and it was my job as her attorney to scramble around, doing whatever I might to preserve some of the assets for his beleaguered wife.

Yet, in the face of disaster, even with the walls around him crumbling, this was not a man who was going to abandon his ways. Fred was intent on trying to salvage some of the money Beth and I had managed to retain for her—this time he was not going to merely steal from strangers, but from her. You may well wonder at Fred's audacity, but it gets better. Who do you think he enlisted to aid him in this scheme?

Their adult son.

By now, you must be saying, "Come on, everyone must have realized he was a crook by that point, especially his family," and you would be right. But the love of a parent is a powerful force. Fred's son grew up idolizing his father, whose life was now in ruins. How could he just walk away, Fred asked his son? Should their son not ask Beth to share some of what she had preserved?

If Beth had not been so understanding, the resentment she would have felt toward her son when he tried to convince her that his father was an honest man and that she should not divorce him, could have been devastating to both of them and, obviously, to their relationship. Fortunately, she was bigger than that. It was difficult for her, but she sat with her son and explained all of the falsehoods, frauds and fakery his father had engaged in—which not only destroyed their family, but also the lives of hundreds of people who had trusted and invested with him. Thankfully, she and her son maintained their closeness, which was especially helpful to him when his father was prosecuted and sent to prison.

The point here is simple. Fred shattered his family, then was willing to ruin what little remained of it because of his selfishness, using his adult son to do his bidding. Reprehensible? Yes, but there is a lesson in this. If you are confronted with a spouse willing to compromise his or her own children in the course of your divorce, write them off, but protect your relationship with those children. Once the divorce is over, they will be the family that remains.

Sally

Sally was overwhelmed with anger when her mother told her she was filing for a divorce. She went on to explain the effect it had on her.

"This presented me with a complete upheaval of all I expected for my future. I didn't know where to turn, tried to find books to help, but they were all filled with obvious advice suited for a moron. I find myself out of control at times, throwing things, sitting, and crying, sometimes, in the car, letting out a blood curdling scream. I think I could have handled it far better when I was a young child. I would have been able to feel I was just like most of my friends whose parents were divorced. I know my grandparents would have helped me through it, but they are all gone now. None of my friends seem to know what to say to me. Both my parents seem to think I should just get over it. I asked Dad if he realized that I was heartbroken and felt betrayed. He said I was a 'big girl' and should be able to accept the reality of life, asking me if I had any idea how defeated he felt by my mother's request to leave. It was clear that they were both consumed by their own feelings and issues, and neither had considered how I might be affected. Maybe that's as it should be, but I have to admit, I felt disappointed and alone."

The feelings generated in the adult child of divorce are complex and should not be treated lightly. Our intention in this chapter is to be sure you are considering the issues your adult child goes through. Sometimes, they need their own outside help from a competent therapist to help cope with the destruction of their family unit. I will provide another example.

<u>John</u>

John said, "I'm really suffering about this divorce. This may sound like I'm only thinking of me, but it's a catastrophic upheaval in my life. I try to understand, but I just don't know where Dad is coming from. He acts as if I should understand why this has come about, but I don't. The other day he actually said to me that at my age and college experiences, I should understand how this can happen, but he will not say what happened, so I am in the dark. And I have no idea what he means about my college experiences. He acts as if I took some course back then about what to do if your parents split up. My emotions are all over the place, I go from pure anger to sorrow. I have a girlfriend, a serious relationship, but now I'm questioning whether our love is real. I thought Mom and Dad were in love and that they would be together forever. My girlfriend and I have talked about getting married next year, but I no longer feel sure. Why get married at all? I actually find myself hating my parents for the divorce. Mom says she now agrees divorce is the right thing, even though she did not at first. I can see the pain it causes her, but I'm not sure about Dad. He seems to be feeling good about it. I need to understand why relationships fall apart, because I would never have predicted it for them, so how do I know about me? It's got me examining my childhood and wondering what I missed, because I thought it was all good. I'm an only child, and now I wonder if that was by design. I never asked."

John's report of what he is going through makes us realize that the adult child of divorce experiences a stream of emotions that cause them to question their feelings and assumptions about the past, not to mention their own commitments. You can hear that John's reactions run the spectrum from anger to sorrow. At times he is filled with rage, while at other times he is steeped in sadness and confusion. He expresses a deep-seated conflict about whether love is ever genuine.

He obviously hates their divorcing but also feels their pain, even though he does not understand why their relationship, which he thought was good, is falling apart.

What is the message from John's experience? In essence, he is telling us that his parents' divorce is leading him to a good deal of introspective analysis, perhaps the most important self- evaluation in which he has ever engaged. Even his confusion and upset about the meaning of love and commitment should not be seen as a negative, but rather as motivation to look inside in ways that may cause him to grow. His message should also help you understand how to deal with your own children, who may be best helped by consulting a psychologist, since it is not the role of either parent to guide him through this.

These cases present just a few examples of how adult children experience their parents' divorce. It is both intuitive and well supported by anecdotal reports as well as research, that adult children of divorce have different issues and concerns than younger children. The key is to remember, whatever their age, that these are still your children and they have all sorts of complex emotions, memories and images of their family and how you all interact. The following are some suggestions about how to deal with issues that may arise:

1. Listen, do not lecture.

The most important thing you can do is to be sure to listen to them when discussing the divorce. Give them the time and space to express how they feel, even if you are uncomfortable with what they are saying. Keep in mind that your divorce is their loss as well as yours.

2. Help them understand that your divorce is not their responsibility.

When talking with younger children, we stress the importance of conveying a key message—that they had nothing to do with your decision to divorce. We have also found that adult children sometimes blame themselves for the family rift. Your task is to disabuse them of any such guilt and remind them that you are both still their parents and want whatever is best for them. Your happiness is up to you, not them.

3. Get along with each other—you are going to continue to be part of their lives.

Weddings, anniversaries, birthdays—there is no escape from the fact that the family goes on for your children even after the divorce is done. Even though adult children will not need much active parenting, it will be helpful to them if the two of you find a way to remain civil toward each other. Whatever arguments you and your ex may need to have, keep them private. Your adult children do not want the two of you to become the types that cannot be in the same room with each other. However combative your divorce may have been, it is over now, and you and your ex-spouse need to behave in a way that will make your children proud and comfortable.

4. Never force your children to take sides.

We have addressed this already, but it is worth saying again. While you may think that only young children can be alienated from their parents, adult children can likewise become estranged. If you complain about your ex to your adult children, because you think "they are adults and can handle it," you are wrong. Believe us, it will end badly for everyone. Even if you find that an adult child tends to take your side without your prompting, be careful to dissuade that sort of partisanship. Take the high road, no matter what has transpired to cause the divorce. Resist saying anything that is detrimental about your ex—remember that is their other parent.

5. Do not use your adult children as your therapist.

Always keep in mind that your adult childrenare not your friends or your therapist, they are your children. Do not dump your feelings, turmoil and worries onto them. They have their own emotions about the divorce with which they will have to deal. Above all, do not share details of what went wrong. It is fine to make clear that certain aspects of the marriage are not their concern.

6. Accentuate the positive, eliminate the negative.

They have their own view of your marriage and the family life they experienced. You cannot rewrite that history, but you can remind them that things were not always unhappy. They may have their own families by now, and they need reassurance that life is not perfect, but the good can greatly exceed the bad. Avoid harping on unpleasant events from the past and recall the fun times whenever possible. Remind them that you and your spouse began your marriage as people who loved each other and that they are the best part of what that union produced, regardless of the differences that led to the divorce. Help them realize that their whole family life was not based on some sort of lie, and that they can create a better destiny for themselves if they are willing to work for it.

8.2 Young and adolescent children of divorce

Now we will talk about the little kids.

Most parents are deeply concerned that a divorce will inevitably damage their young children. Quite the contrary, as many studies show that when parents are engaged in a high level of conflict during the marriage, their children actually do better *after* their parents' divorce. In most cases, once they have ended their negative marital relationship, mothers and fathers are better able to engage in a positive way with their children. Many even find they have a greater degree of involvement and hands-on-parenting than when they were married. A bad marriage tends to take time and energy as battles are being waged, rather than devoting that time to the children.

You may also fear the consequences of time apart from your children, particularly if you are not the prime custodial parent. Researchers have also found that worry to be unfounded. A recent study showed that being away from one of the parents for periods of time, even one or two weeks, did not affect the mental health or development of the children, nor did it impact their feelings for the parent they are not seeing as much.*

There are certainly problems that arise if one of the parents interferes with the visitation rights of the other, or when a child is rejecting contact with one of the parents. This can be harmful and painful for the child as well as to the rejected mother or father. If this occurs, the healthiest approach is for both parents to assess the damage being done by their behavior and determine what is creating this opposition in the child. This is a time to examine what messages are being given and the quality of the general interaction that exists in the home of the "rejected parent." Very often, when a child resists being with one parent, the issue results from how the adults are communicating. Remember this—you have ended your marriage relationship with your children's other parent, which may have involved years of strife, but it is essential that the negativity does not carry over to how the two of you now relate to the children.

This is a time for deep soul searching.

When things are handled properly, studies by the National Institutes of Health show that children of divorce tend to be "more open to communication."* When the post-divorce relationship is not hostile, your children will have a renewed opportunity to flourish.

A Dartmouth study on the effects of divorce on children, using 2,500 subjects, reported that "75-80 percent of the children develop into well-adjusted adults with no lasting psychological or behavioral problems."* In addition, they reported that children of divorce tend to achieve their education and career goals and manifest the ability to build close relationships.

Our experience when working with parents going through a divorce is that one of their biggest concerns is to figure out how to make sure the kids are okay. Keep in mind, as you think about your children, the issue of their well-being is not whether a divorce occurred, but how well the parents handle that process; how they maintain the meaning of family; and whether the parents make an effort to keep the idea of LOVE for their children intact.

It may not be an original thought, but it is critical—the message that you will always love your children, even though you and your spouse could not make your marriage work, must be provided on an ongoing basis.

The effect of a divorce on children will vary from case to case, there is no set pattern. You must be prepared for any of the possible responses. Some children react in an understanding way while others seem to struggle. However, most children are resilient and, if the situation is handled in a good way, they can experience the divorce as an adjustment to their life rather than a crisis. Much of their reaction is a function of their individual temperaments, age and, of course, the way the situation is presented and handled by the parents.

When children are put in the middle of ongoing anger between their parents, the problems will be obvious, particularly in terms of their social development. Children in that situation will typically have a harder time relating to others because they feel insecure—family and love should provide a solid foundation, not uncertainty.

During conversations with your children about the split, it helps to mention other families, to assure them that divorce is not some rare and evil event. If possible, refer to the children from other divorced families who are happy and have a good life. It will be helpful if both parents are present for the initial conversation when the children are told of the divorce. The important thing to communicate is that this is not an uncommon happening and, most important, that they are in no way responsible for the separation and divorce.

One of the *musts* when speaking with your children about the divorce, is that anger is never displayed. When children witness anger between their parents during these talks, they themselves may become angry or irritable. When parents find they are so locked into feelings of anger toward each other that they are unable to hide from the children, it is critical for them to seek counseling to work through this dilemma.

Another critical rule for these interactions, is that guilt be avoided as a topic or even a thought. Children try to make sense out of why the divorce is happening, and it is common for them to assume some guilt for what is happening. Children can become caught up in concerns about having done poorly in school or sports, or otherwise having upset their parents. Some believe that the angry reactions from their parents provoked by these failings might have played some part in the decision to end the marriage. Any such tendency must be dealt with early on. There must be an effort by both parents to make clear the children played no role in the decision, and that the divorce is strictly because of feelings between the parents. Giving direct statements that your children did not cause the rift will help children eliminate any feelings of guilt. Researchers emphasize that this is an excellent time for both parents to re-enforce an attitude of love and unconditional positive regard toward their children.

Just as partners going through a divorce experience several various emotions, anxiety, and confusion, it is important to accept that your children are no different. Even when the presentation and follow-up behaviors are done well, they will certainly have to wrestle with their own issues. For instance, children often feel overwhelmed and vulnerable. They will need an outlet to express their reactions—someone to talk to, someone who will listen, and ideally this should be their parents. In some cases, it will be valuable to have them see a psychologist, even just a few times, for support and understanding.

The following are some general guidelines for parents to consider in handling their children during and after divorce:*

1. Children should be involved in making the decisions as to the best alternate visiting and living arrangements with the separated parents.
2. No matter how tense the situation, anger between the parents should never be expressed in front of the children. Parents should be constantly vigilant about this, since anger is often the default reaction to disagreements between former spouses.
3. There should never be any comments made to the child about how the other parent is parenting.

4. The children should never be present when parents are debating any aspect of interacting with the children.

5. Each parent must encourage their children to honestly express their feelings about how their life is going during and after the divorce. Children need to know that their feelings are important and will be considered seriously.

6. Encourage the children to put their feelings into words. Parents should be aware that children often have difficulty verbalizing their emotions and they should be encouraged to express what they are feeling.

7. With patience and reassurance, your children will be fine despite the divorce. Their tensions and anxieties will be minimized through your understanding and acknowledgment that they feel their life has been turned up-side-down.

8. Try to provide routines that replicate their life before the divorce. When they feel they can rely on the routines that are most important to them, it will convey stability, structure, and ongoing caring.

9. Do your best to maintain a working relationship with your former spouse. As already stated, do all you can to avoid your children witnessing any conflict between you and your former spouse.

10. Provide a continuing sense of support, from both of you, to help them get through this unsettling time. It will communicate that they are loved by both parents and will create an even closer bond to both.

11. Be sure to make it clear you are staying involved in their life at all times. You can set up email, text, and phone schedules so you remain in contact when they are with the other parent. Both parents staying involved in their life conveys a regard to them that can be as important as love during this period.

12. Never do anything to make them feel they have to take sides. If possible, say only kind things to your children about the other parent. If you cannot bring yourself to say positive things, say nothing.

13. When children relate some favorable experience with the other parent, as difficult as it may be, avoid showing any jealousy or any put down of the good time the children are relating. Thoughts such as, "She doesn't work, so of course she has all the time in the world to take them to see that movie," must be kept to yourself and not vocalized in front of the children.
14. Avoid any comments of blaming the other parent for the divorce. Divorce should be viewed as a modeling for your children on handling conflict and adversity in life.
15. Be ever aware that children react to divorce in different ways. A common expression you may hear from them is that they feel like they've done something to cause the divorce. This theme is a totally normal reaction in many children and your job is to repeatedly assure them that they are not in any way responsible and, in fact, played no role in the divorce decision.

One valuable lesson your children can learn through divorce is that some problems cannot be solved, and that it is possible to reach a peaceful disengagement from conflict and pain. Whatever you may think, it is likely that your children were well aware from an early age that their parents were not getting along very well. A bad marital relationship is an unhappy situation for the entire family. Once that is acknowledged, a divorce communicates that people do not have to settle for unhappiness. Many children we have counseled expressed the wish their parents had divorced earlier, instead of fighting all the time. A study done at the University of Notre Dame revealed that parents who regularly demonstrated their anger toward each other in front of their children, may well have been setting those children up for depression, anxiety and behavioral problems.*

You have taken the journey to Splitsville in search of freedom, happiness, and new relationships, which should be made apparent to your children. Along the way, we know you will also be mindful of all of their needs.

8.3 Talking to your ex about the children

If you have children, communicating with your ex about visitation schedules, education, financial matters, and various other parenting issues is unavoidable. You may wish that by the time you reach Splitsville you will be done with your ex, but that is never reality, especially when you have children together. Talking about them and their issues is not optional. And be prepared- do not fool yourself into thinking this will only be true while they are young, because it is never going to end. It may not be easy, but it is a main component in helping your children cope, and even to aid you in moving on with your new life.

One of the primary reasons you had for dissolving the marriage may have been a desire to protect your children from the negative relationship between you and your spouse. So, do not defeat this purpose of the divorce by engaging in an ongoing battle with your ex about them. It is obviously best for both parents to agree on keeping the interactions as benign as possible, but if your ex refuses to cooperate, then you need to be the bigger person and KEEP YOUR CHILDREN OUT OF HARM'S WAY.

Whether your discussions with your ex are polite or angry, be sure the children cannot overhear them. Avoid any unpleasant interactions in front of them. It is sad to admit, but there are ex-spouses who find it impossible to communicate without conflict. If you are stuck in that situation, find an independent person, preferably a therapist, to help with the discussions and decisions that have to be made.

We realize it is easy to suggest these things, but difficult to put them in place. You've gone through all sorts of upset in divorcing, and now we are asking you to be civil with the person you see as responsible for the trauma. BUT YOU NEED TO DO IT. All of the research in this area emphatically shows that denigrating your ex to your children will have a detrimental effect on your children's mental health and their ability to adjust to the divorce. Your children have to discover for themselves the positive and negative features of both parents. It is not your job to criticize your ex. Your goal should be to show them the best YOU possible. Well supported psychological research indicates that your children will make their own decisions about each parent.

Soon after or during the divorce process, most parents report that communication around the children was not smooth and it took great restraint on their part to keep it positive. The good news is that research shows that most parents eventually find a way to communicate with each other that is not hostile and loaded with conflictual anger. This does not mean they become the best of friends, but at least they are no longer screaming curses at each other and realize that the children's well-being is the basic goal for both of them.

Dealing with your ex about your children will not be among your favorite things to do. The following are some tips on how to interact with your ex around child issues without starting a war or resorting to alcohol.

1. Keep it Brief.

When discussing your children with your ex, be sure to have a plan, say what you want, and then STOP! The less you ramble on, the less chance that the interaction will end up in an argument. Keep in mind the topics and nature of the disagreements you had while married and avoid replicating them.

2. Choose The Time Of Conversing--- To Your Advantage.

Do not call or accept calls from your ex if you have just had a rough time with something, if you are tired, or if you are generally in a bad mood. Schedule conversations with your ex when you feel rested, in control and energetic.

3. Be Prepared.

Suppose your ex chooses to just walk into your home uninvited without calling. or calls you at the most inconvenient times. Do not hesitate to say that this is not a good time or that you are not ready to discuss any co-parenting issues. It is difficult for anyone to think under pressure, so do not allow yourself to be put in that position. Set your boundaries, including restrictions on your ex coming in the house, and know how you will respond if your ex tries to push things to his/her advantage.

4. Avoid Attacking, Name Calling, And Labeling.

Stay away from saying anything about your ex's appearance, your opinion of their lifestyle, how they are handling finances, and especially the time spent with the children. Avoid any inquiries or comments about their relationships. The basic principle to follow is that no matter how curious you are, or how much you object to something, your life and your children's adjustment will be best served if you bite your tongue about those things.

5. It Is Not Your Job To Teach Parenting.

This may be difficult to accept, but your ex has the right to parent the way they see fit and believe is right for your children. You may not agree with their style, but insisting your way is best is a value judgement that is tainted by the elements of a marriage gone wrong. Some children are quite adept at manipulating their parents to get what they want by complaining about the other parent. If you feel there is a serious issue with some aspect of your ex's parenting, stay away from personal attacks and, if necessary, seek professional help from a counsellor or attorney.

6. No Blaming.

Avoid the temptation to blame your ex if the children get into some sort of trouble on their watch. Blame is a toxic emotion and will not help to resolve the child issue. Instead, examine the situation from all sides and be sure it is as urgent or important as you first thought.

7. Keep Humanism In The Equation.

The fact remains that your ex is your children's other parent. Your ex may have made a terrible marriage partner, but they are going to continue to be in the lives of you and your children, so provide the appropriate measure of respect—no matter how much you hate them.

8.4 Legal implications of divorce on child support, education, and parenting

Needless to say, this is an area of great concern for any divorcing parent. Since rules vary from state to state, this is also something for which you will need experienced advice from your attorney or, if you have proceeded to mediation without counsel, then from the mediator.

In some states, there are specific guidelines that help calculate appropriate child support based on the number of children and the respective income of the two parties. You can find those online without too much difficulty, but they will not solve all of your problems even if that matrix exists in your jurisdiction. In addition, many of these charts only go as high as a relatively modest income level and further input will be required. The key here, harking back to the financial affidavit you created, is to make a fair assessment of what you will need to live after the divorce has been concluded, including the expenses required to support the children.

Along with this comes the matter of education, where there is a huge spectrum of variables. Are your children in public school, private school or parochial school? Do you expect them to go to college and, if so, will you opt for your state universities, which are typically less expensive, or can you afford to send them to a private college either in or out of your state? What sort of extracurricular activities have they been involved in up to now and which of them will you be able to afford to continue? Sports teams? Piano lessons? Art classes? Dance lessons?

Whatever the answers to these questions may be, you should work hard not to allow your children to be cheated in any way as a result of their parents' marriage having failed. The emotional impact of the divorce will be enough for them to cope with. They are going to have to learn new ways of interacting with each parent. Spending nights in the home of the non-custodial parent and away from their normal routine. Meeting new people whom either or both of their parents may be dating. While you are going through the massive upheaval that divorce causes, there are obviously going to be an array of issues for your children to face. Do not exacerbate the situation by depriving them in any way of the things from which they derive the most pleasure in their academic and after-school activities.

As with most things you will be facing on the road to Splitsville, a lot will depend on how you and your spouse relate to each other, your children, and your overall circumstances. If you and your spouse can work together for the benefit of your children then you should be applauded, and you may find that it will assist in your post-divorce dealings with each other. Conversely, if your spouse is selfish and cares only for himself or herself, then you must shoulder more of the burden of normalizing life for your children than would otherwise be fair.

But you can do it.

As a loving parent, we believe you will do what is best for your children, even if it sometimes means sacrificing things for yourself. And we are not just talking about material things. Far more important is the time and energy you will be asked to devote to your sons and daughters, because they are being carried along on this journey without having anything to say about it, whether they like it or not. Please never forget that, not even in those difficult moments when all you want to do is shut your bedroom door, turn off the lights, turn on the television, lay back on your bed and zone out. Your children are going to need you and you will feel better in the end if you are there for them even when it is the most difficult for you.

To that end, we are going to discuss some of the issues you will face as parents. This is by no means comprehensive, but we promise that we have done our best to consider all of the major categories with which we have had experience.

8.5 Coparenting and scheduling

Adjusting from an intact family to two separate co-parenting homes is usually not an easy transition and in almost all cases presents issues for both parents. Agreeing on a schedule that permits the children to be with each of you is one of the most important interactions you and your ex must have very soon after a divorce. All of the research literature in this area is definite in stressing the importance of children being assured that they will spend equal time with each parent, if that is their expressed wish. Although this is usually desired by both parents the situation can become complicated by issues such as the two of you not living close to each other, not yet arranged school events, medical appointments, holidays, bedtimes, eating habits and the children's social calendar.

If you and your ex share a good healthy co-parenting relationship, both of you will avoid any intention to manipulate your ex and will not try to control the children's allegiances. No matter how antagonistic the marital and divorce relationship was, it is essential to acknowledge that it's best for the children to have a good relationship with both parents and they should never feel that there is competition between parents for their affection and commitment.

<u>Harry</u>

Harry explained that he always hears his parents argue about how the other one acts with us when at their house. Mom gets upset, real crazy, because Dad lets us stay up until nine at night. Mom insists that eight is our bedtime and she has this strange belief that we are, in her words, grumpy the next day if we don't get enough sleep. She's nuts about bedtime. She thinks the one hour more at Dad's house is making us brats. We go back and forth from mom to dad every Wednesday night and stay with that parent until Saturday morning. It's a real pain in the you know what. I wish we could just stay in either place for one whole week. I'm eight and my sister, Lil, is twelve. Lil doesn't talk much, but I know she complains to me that she never gets to spend time with her friends on Saturday because the whole day is taken up by packing to go back and waiting to get picked up. Another thing, neither mom nor dad is ever on time to get us and always have some excuse we are supposed to understand and they want us to say, That's ok. Mom not only thinks Dad lets us stay up too late, but she also yells at him for letting us play our video games. I hate to listen to them talk on the phone, so I go to the basement when she calls him. He's much tougher than she knows and we have to clean the house when we stay with him. As soon as she gets us in the car, we hear that we should stay home with her because he is not good for us and doesn't know how to take care of us. I think she's, you know, loony. (Makes a corkscrew sign at the temple of his head). Lil has told me she doesn't know why they don't ask us about what visitation schedule we would like. I agree with Lil. They leave us out of all the decisions about what we do. Last week mom decided I needed a haircut and made an appointment with her hairdresser lady. She did not ask me or dad if we thought I needed a haircut. She just took me to her lady hairdresser and now I'm almost bald. Dad thinks it's wrong and told me he did not think I should be forced to cut my hair. He says he thinks it looked fine.

You can hear in Harry's reflections on what he and Lil feel about how their parents arranged scheduling and basically on how they hate to hear judgmental and negative comments about the other parent. Children usually put a great value on being included in decisions about them and particularly about visitation scheduling.

Cindy

Cindy, a sixteen- year- old girl, said that her father had arranged for her to have counseling because she told him what her mother was saying about him when she and her sister are with her at her house.

"You want to hear the kind of things she says?" she asked. "I have heard this from my mom a million times. She says we will eventually see through him and realize he is a sick man and doesn't know how to love. He's not giving her enough money to live on and we can't go on any vacations this year because of him. He wanted the divorce, it's his fault, she didn't want to get divorced. He was out with another woman, while she was home with us every night. He tries to make you think he loves you but believe me, after all these years with him, I can tell you he does not know what love is. When you visit with him he gets prepared food for you for supper, at the deli and tells you it's because he gets home too late to cook. That's bullshit. He just doesn't want to be bothered cooking for you. Be careful, he's a con artist. I know, I lived with him all those years and he will use you against me any time he can."

Cindy stopped, took a deep breath, then added, "I feel like she's put a knife in my stomach every time she trash talks about my dad that way. I love him and I feel like he loves me, no matter what she says."

These two reports from children, regarding one parent "trash talking" about the other parent, are presented to help you understand that your children are clearly affected in a major way when you berate the other parent. The following is a collection of comments I made over years of practice when I asked children of divorced families and what they would like to say to their parents:

"Why can't you two get along and stop fighting? Stop putting us in the middle of your anger toward each other. You are really taking out your anger about dad/mom, by telling me all these bad things. Can't you two stop fighting, even divorced? Hey, how about our feelings? You guys are making us cry at night. We don't want to hear about money. We are not your spies."

The message we need to convey to you, is for you to be aware of how very important it is to avoid making disparaging remarks about your children's other parent. Saying unkind things about your ex, particularly about their parenting roles, will most likely upset the children and hurt their feelings. Accept the widely validated fact that most children love both parents, regardless of the shortcomings or flaws the parents they may have. Therefore, if you say unkind things about your ex, regardless of how accurate you think it may be, those comments usually hurt your children. Children, usually after the age of five or six, are well aware that they are the product of both of their parents. In the children's interpretation, when you say negative things about their parent you are, to them, saying those same things about them.

We understand that curbing your comments when your ex gets you angry can be most difficult. However, we can assure you that inhibiting your negative comments or as the children often call it, "trash talk," will really create a much more positive relationship between you and your ex and especially between your children and both of you. Think of it this way!

Every time your children think they are hearing this "trash talk" from one of you about the other parent, it chips away at their own self-esteem.

The process of conversing with your ex about the children in a civil manner in many ways depends on how you judge your interaction in this realm. Too often, the baggage of hostility and poor communication that went on in the marriage is carried over to post-divorce conversations with the ex.

The following is a questionnaire designed for you to assess your behavior. Since there is little you can do to change the behavior of your ex, at least you can try to improve the situation. Read the statements below and answer true or false for each. Try not to give it too much thought, just provide your honest, instinctive responses:

1. I believe I am trying to be a good parent.
2. I ask my ex their opinion on issues related to parenting.
3. I acknowledge my ex when they pay the right amount of attention to our children.
4. I acknowledge it when my ex spends quality time with our children.
5. When we talk about the children, I feel my ex and I have the same goals for them.
6. I do my best to be a responsible parent.
7. I allow for the fact that my ex and I have different ideas about how to raise our children.
8. I tell my ex they are doing a good job as a parent.
9. We often get into a good discussion about how to best meet our children's needs.
10. I admit it when my ex shows that they are willing to make personal sacrifices to help take care of our children.
11. I allow for the fact that my ex and I have different ideas about the routines our children should follow.

12. I do not make jokes or sarcastic comments about the way my ex is as a parent.
13. I can tell from our interactions that my ex does not trust my abilities as a parent.
14. I pick up signs that my ex has developed some sensitivity to the children's feelings and needs that was not present before.
15. It has become clearer since the divorce that we have different standards for our children's behavior.
16. I feel that my ex does not carry his/ her fair share of the parenting work.
17. I feel that my ex is trying to undermine my parenting.
18. I feel conversations with my ex are helping us to grow and mature together by revealing to each other our experiences as a parent.
19. When I feel at my wits end, my ex seems to find ways to increase my stress.
20. The stress of co-parenting has caused my ex and me to grow even further apart.

Now that you have given your answers, please look back. You will know what is right and wrong and that the proper path will become clear to you.

Types of Schedules

We often get questions about what are the possible co-parenting schedules that seem to work best for the children. Most of the time a 50/50 co-parenting schedule works best There is no question that the best schedule is never the same for every family. Accept that after putting in a great deal of energy in establishing what is the best schedule for you and your ex to follow, it may need to change as the children get older and get involved in different activities and commitments. No matter what changes occur, always focus on creating a schedule that puts the children first in their needs to live within events that are important to them.

The benefit of a routine with frequent parenting time exchanges is that parents and children get to spend time together more frequently. Yet it can be difficult for parents who don't live very close to transport their children between homes. Moreover, children who have difficulty making frequent transitions may have a hard time with a routine that is based on changing visitation sites too often.

Parents understand the needs of their children better than anyone and it's essential that they use that knowledge to craft an ideal parenting schedule that caters to those needs before anything else. While the task may be to divide parenting responsibilities across their two homes, working together to make these decisions for the children is an excellent foot to start on in co-parenting.

A one-size-fits-all parenting schedule does not exist, but there are a few routines commonly used by parents that cater to many different family situations. If you and your co-parent are working out parenting time and scheduling logistics, one of these routines could be a good pattern for your family to follow. Here are just a few:

BI-WEEKLY SCHEDULE:

A biweekly parenting schedule allows the children to spend one entire week living with each parent at a time. This routine could make a good fit for older children with busier schedules or when parents live in the same town.

TWO WEEKS AGREEMENT:

Some families report that the children feel less disruption if instead of going back and forth every other week, they like staying with one parent for two weeks at a time. Many children prefer this reduced number of shifts from house to house. Where the parents live and what school the children attend is critical as with all of these options.

EXTENDED WEEKEND SCHEDULE:

The extended weekend schedule permits children to spend weekdays with one parent and a long weekend (or every other weekend) with the other parent. This works well where the parents live in different towns and the children need a regular base from where they can get to school.

8.6 Talking to your ex about money

If there is anything worse than a discussion with your ex about an amicable visitation schedule, it is dealing with financial issues, especially those that are child based. Unfortunately, it is not unusual to find yourself having these conversations with your ex long after the divorce is finalized, especially if you had children together.

Talking with your ex about money matters is often a highly charged subject, since so much of that ties into the way in which your marriage was finished. As soon as the topic of money rears its ugly head, some people find that any goodwill or cooperation that had been built between the parties seems to evaporate. If you find yourself in this unpleasant space, it may help if you understand why the conflict over money has such a high emotional charge—other than the obvious, which is, it is about *money*!

First, there is a natural animosity because one of you is asking for money from the other, and the one being asked may believe they have already given too much. Then there is the issue about how the money will actually be spent. There may be a woman asking for money to buy the children sneakers, while the husband wonders if some or all of it might be spent on her own hairdresser, clothing, or some activity she cannot otherwise afford. We have all heard divorced people complain that they are being asked to, "Toss money down the toilet, flushing it away and never knowing where the hell it went."

Or what about the debate that turns into an argument over whether your daughter needs dance lessons or your son needs piano lessons or some other extra-curricular item you might not have considered in the fine print of your Separation Agreement. Then there is the mother who is struggling to create a comfortable life for herself and her children while she hears about her newly single husband going out on dates with a string of women he met online or, worse, that old friends introduced him to.

We have already examined the things you will need to deal with in creating your new life. In this section, we are focusing on post-divorce finances, and we believe it is not difficult to engage in those money conversations without signaling the start of a new World War. We will proceed on the assumption that the large majority of these disputes and discussions will involve the children, since the financial terms of the split from your ex should have been clearly spelled out. If that is not the case, we will deal with that at the end of this section.

Empower your ex.

If you are the primary caregiver for your children, then you are the one who manages the money that your ex contributes. That is at the root of the potential problem in money discussions and decisions. Whether you empathize with this or not, it is disempowering for your ex to just hand over money and not have any involvement in how the children are being supported. Since the two of you have divorced, we think it is fair to say that there is a limit on trust, and a natural assumption that the money being requested is unreasonable.

Try to overcome this initial barrier by working to empower your ex. Steer the conversation toward the lives of your children. Let your ex know precisely what is going on, what they are doing, and how money is being spent. Involve your ex in their activities, whether it be sports, artistic endeavors or whatever else your ex may participate in or simply attend.

Structuring the money discussion in this way should turn it from a one-sided demand into a mutual review of how things should be handled.

Some of you may be saying, "But I hate the sonuvabitch and don't want them at my son's baseball games or my daughter's ballet recitals." Not fair and, more important, not healthy for the children. Whatever kind of rotten jerk your ex is—unless there is molestation or abuse involved—they will benefit from both parents being involved in their activities and lives.

Establish and maintain ground rules.

Remember to conduct all interactions with your ex as if they are non-emotional business meetings. This is especially essential in discussions about money. So, strip out the emotions from the discussion and absolutely avoid name calling and accusations. Never bring up how much better the financial situation would be if your ex had done or not done certain things. You should never say, for example, things like, "If you hadn't invested in that paper stock company, we would be a lot richer than we are," or "If you listened to me the last time you did your taxes, you would not have the debt you have." As we all know, these accusations may feel good, but they will lead to problems in moving toward what you are hoping to accomplish. Always try to stay focused on the specific purpose of the interaction.

Use the "Question Technique" (with respect to Socrates).

Instead of opening the conversation with a statement that your son, Jake, needs money for a math tutor or football helmet, start the conversation with a question of your ex, such as saying, "Jake thinks he needs a math tutor because he is failing math. How do you feel about him getting one?" If you start the conversation with a question instead of a statement of need, your ex will have a chance to process the request and the need of the situation, rather than just focus on the money issue. You might also add something like, "I've tried to help him with the math, but that's really your area and it's beyond me." You are giving your ex a role in addressing Jake's need, perhaps even setting it up so that the ex feels it's a joint decision, rather than just a demand for money. The style of asking, how do you feel about that, makes it a question rather than a demand. Psychologically you are priming the ex to see things from the perspective of the child and you are acknowledging that you are willing to do the same. You may not realize it, but this is an empathic communication style. You're priming your ex to see things from your perspective by letting him/her know that you're willing to do the same. "Empathy is what drives good outcomes."

Never open with a demand.

Try to open your financial discussion with an invitation approach and never with a demand. For example, never start by saying, "I need more money for Jake." Instead, start by explaining Jake's situation. Consider the following example of using invitation rather than a "demand" for more money:

"Jake is doing really well in football, and the helmet you bought him is great. It seems to give him the best protection. He is doing so well that he made the regional travel team, which means he has to stay overnight in a motel with the team. It's getting expensive and I wanted to give you an opportunity to think about it because I do not have enough money in the budget to cover all the expenses."

This approach is more than just declaring the need for more money. It again puts your ex in the position of deciding if he/she wants to give Jake this opportunity. This approach further communicates your appreciation that it might be something the co-parent wants to think about and that you accept that as an important step for him/her.

Do not forget to acknowledge the good things.

Letting your ex know that you appreciate the child support which he/she has contributed to will go a long way to getting your financial needs accomplished. Whenever possible, begin the conversation with gratefulness for what your co-parent has already done before discussing additional expenses. Saying things like, "I really appreciate your covering the bill for Jake's football equipment, and I am sure to tell him that you bought it for him." Focus on showing gratitude rather than becoming defensive or just telling your ex you need more money for something.

Use the "Fairness Approach".

This is a tough one, since the last thing in the world you may feel toward your ex is "fairness," but it does work and it will help *you.*

The technique of asking what your ex thinks is fair to contribute to a certain need can go a long way toward reaching an agreeable financial arrangement. It can also preempt friction. It gives your ex a chance to voice his/her opinion and preference first and helps in coming up with a compromised solution.

8.7 Living together after the divorce.

In recent years, there has been an increase in the number of couples opting to live together for some period of time after they divorce. Very often, this results from financial considerations; or needing time to sell the house and divide the proceeds before moving on separately; or some concern about their children; or any one of a number of other reasons.

The truth, in our experience, is that this choice can be difficult for the parties to handle and often ends up with stormy waters ahead and an unpleasant finish. Continuing to reside in the same home, albeit in separate bedrooms, while one or both of you is pursuing their newfound independence, can create serious tension for all involved.

Some money can certainly be saved in the short term by maintaining a single household. By now, you have realized that divorce, in and of itself, is costly, and it is natural to try and figure out ways to economize. Unfortunately, the notion of living together is often poorly thought out or planned and it soon becomes obvious that the various negative aspects of your relationship have not been resolved.

Couples are making a different sort of mistake if they live together post-divorce because they believe it will be easier for their children and help their youngsters avoid the detrimental effects of divorce. As discussed elsewhere, when it comes to children, the best thing that you can do is remove them from the battleground that your marriage became.

Remaining together after the divorce involves a new set of problems, as you will have to come to agreement on any number of issues. Reaching that accord is tough enough, but sticking to it will be even more difficult. Remember, you made a decision to END THE RELATIONSHIP. It should be obvious that jumping back into some modified version of that arrangement is not a great idea.

You got all the way to Splitsville. You should savor your freedom. Explore new opportunities. Live your life on your own terms. And here is the big one, MEET NEW PEOPLE. Is it logical to believe you are going to be able to do all that with your ex-spouse two rooms away? Divorce is a process intended to provide you separate lives. You can see how living together, no matter how well-intended, is going to interfere with what you should be pursuing and enjoying.

Nevertheless, you may feel this is something you have to do, at least for a while, for one reason or another. If so, there are several specific areas that tend to become most problematic in this situation, which we will address here:

Sharing resources.

Sharing resources would seem to be one of the easiest areas to agree upon and one that makes the arrangement economically sensible. However, resources are not just financial—they include time, commitment to a style of life, and just about everything else that defines your existence. The ability to agree upon and then honor the commitment of those resources is not easily negotiated and maintained.

You are the same people after divorce as you were in the marriage, especially when it involves how the two of you interact. If one of you never washed a dish, did the laundry, or took out the garbage, how much change do you think you will see now that you're legally split?

In marriage, there was a common bag of resources and responsibilities that have now morphed into two separate stashes. How generous are you going to be feeling toward your ex-spouse? How do you think they feel about you?

If you have concluded that co-habiting for some time is unavoidable after the divorce, here is our advice: BE REALISTIC. If you couldn't count on your spouse when you were married, expect even less now.

Other relationships and your hope to be moving on.

It is not difficult to see that living with your former spouse will have a chilling effect on your efforts to build other relationships—particularly those of the romantic variety. The added dimension here comes from the natural jealousy one of you will feel when you see the other forming alternative relationships. Resentment will ensue, along with uncomfortable interactions with the third parties involved. Living together after divorce can become a barrier to forming new friends and can become an anguishing and difficult process. In this situation, the conflict you felt in the marriage is likely to increase rather change in a positive direction.

Not only will it create a new level of tension between you and your ex-spouse, but how do you think the other person will feel when they learn the identity of your roommate? As you establish a new life after divorce, you are going to find someone else with whom you want to form a close bond and maybe even an intimate relationship. Think of the effect on that person, knowing you are still living with your former spouse. Your new friend may come to doubt that you have truly given up your "first love," and you may be risking that new relationship. Consider how living together after divorce may be some sort of denial that you have accepted the split.

What will the rest of the world think?

The way you are viewed by others inevitably plays a role shaping your future. If you decide to live together after ending the marriage, it will be essential that you discuss and agree upon how this is being presented to the people in your world. Many prefer to keep their agreement private to lessen the questions asked and to diminish the effect it might have in social groups and even at work.

Managing how your children see this arrangement.

Despite ending your marital partnership, living in the same house means that no matter how you arrange it, you will see each other every day, you will share some common space and there will be some level of ongoing interaction with the person you were determined to get away from.

Your child's life will be even more complicated when parents live together after divorce, making the adjustment much more difficult. No matter how the parents rationalize the situation it will be confusing to children. Are their parents divorced or are they not? Some children may think of this arrangement as a sham. Worse yet, if the children are encouraged to keep this situation a secret. Parents should never teach their children it is all right to lie!

Then there are the practical aspects of what your children will witness. Their parents, sleeping in separate rooms, never showing love or affection towards each other. Partners who divorce and live apart give their children the opportunity to carve out a new relationship with each of them in a healthy, positive way.

CHAPTER 9
THE PATH TO HAPPINESS

"The best way to predict your future is to create it." —Abraham Lincoln

It is our sincere hope that we have assisted you in navigating the road to Splitsville. Once you reach the conclusion of your divorce, the logical question is:

What next?

We trust that you have completed the exercises we provided; have had a good look at who you are; have a full understanding of what led you into your marriage; have a clear picture of what caused the end of your marriage; and that you are now ready to move ahead.

But you may feel you have arrived at a daunting place.

Just like any major event to which you have devoted a lot of emotion and effort, once it is over there is an inevitable sense of emptiness. Think, for instance, about how you felt at the end of a large party you created and hosted. Or after a wonderful vacation. Or after all of the Christmas or Hanukah presents have been opened, the dinner is done, and the dishes put away.

You may sit on your couch, take a deep breath, and wonder:

What next?

This is especially true once the gavel has come down on your marriage and you find yourself single and, possibly, alone. Even if you have prepared for that let down, that sense of decompression, you must not allow yourself to be consumed by it.

This chapter is intended to guide you along a new road, a journey beyond Splitsville—the Path to Happiness.

Assuming your divorce is final, you are confronting the reality that things will never be the same again. There are various possible reactions possible, all of which are completely normal. For some, this finality comes as a shock, while others feel an overwhelming sense of relief.

Some are frightened, others happy, some exhilarated, others sad. For many, it is a combination of these emotions.

Whatever you are feeling, the best thing you can do is to initiate changes in your life— as soon as possible. Do not allow yourself to become paralyzed as you stare at the empty spaces in your life once occupied by your ex-partner. Your world has not come to an end… it is only beginning!

We are going to help steer you in the right direction, onto this new path, taking simple but concrete steps to find your new self as well as a renewed sense of passion. We are going to help you reignite your positive energy and ward off all the pain and drama you had to deal with during your divorce. We want to help you gain confidence as you construct a new, healthier and happier version of yourself.

So, take a deep breath, hold your head high, and embrace the excitement of knowing that you are about to create the life you want and deserve.

Let's get started.

9.1 Begin your path to happiness with the correct attitude and the right questions.

Inspiration

Inspiration is a simple but powerful word. We know from experience with hundreds of divorced people that your life at this point can use some perking up and the key to that is feeling *inspired.* You need to fight fear, lethargy and doubt.

A divorce can very easily leave you with negative feelings about yourself. Becoming inspired will help lift you out of these heartfelt blues.

You need to get off the couch and on your feet, literally and figuratively. We know this can be easier said than done, but inspirational forces are everywhere if you allow yourself to recognize them. We will help point them out.

Aspiration

Aspiration is another important concept that will help you build the life you deserve. By that, we mean that you should identify the dreams and hopes you have for your future. Only then can you *aspire* to reach them. There are many different types of aspirations, including those involving social, career, financial and personal aspects of your life. Aspiration should be thought of as a way of reaching for the stars, about creating the life you want and deserve.

We will help you look at what you want and what goals you should be establishing as you build your new life—free of the mistakes you made in the past.

Inertia

People tend to remember that Sir Isaac Newton "discovered" gravity when the apple fell on his head as he relaxed beneath a tree. But they tend to forget that he also formulated the theory of inertia—that a body in motion tends to stay in motion, while a body at rest tends to stay at rest.

"What has that got to do with me?" you may ask. "Do I need a physics lesson?"

The answer is simple. If you keep sitting on that couch, agonizing over the divorce you have just endured and agonizing about what will become of you, then you are experiencing the fate of a body at rest. That is what is called *inertia* and you need to break the pattern and get moving.

Having said that, we realize how tough it can be to get you going on the path we want you to take. But once you begin, once you have been *inspired* to seek your new happiness and begin to *aspire* to the things you want and deserve for your life, then you have begun your journey on the path to happiness. That is called momentum and that is when *inertia* will work for you rather than against you. Remember the second part of Newton's axiom—a body in motion tends to keep going—so get off the couch and get going!

What questions are you asking yourself?

It is not unusual, once you have split, to dwell on the past. We have already addressed this in various ways, but it is worth noting again. You may well find yourself asking, "How did I end up in such a lousy relationship?" or "Why me?" or "How did things go wrong?" or "Why did I put up with it for so long?"

We have spent a lot of time emphasizing the notion that there is value in understanding why your marriage failed and why you got divorced. You have patiently gone through that with us and you are here now. You made it to Splitsville. Further dwelling on negative self- chatter is not going to lead you on your new journey to happiness. Instead of focusing on a wide variety of unhelpful hand-wringing, how about WE ask YOU a question—

> Do you think any of those thoughts are helpful, productive or likely to lead you to future happiness?
>
> Of course not.
>
> In life, the type and quality of questions you ask yourself will inevitably affect the way you live, so let's start with some positive inquiries, beginning with—
>
> What sort of life do you want?

That question is something each of us thinks about from time to time, but now that you have arrived at Splitsville, this is YOUR time to ask! This is the time to pull out your notebook and pen—yes, sorry, one last list—and write down all of your dreams, big and small. You cannot achieve what you want in life without taking some time to identify your goals. Act INSPIRED and be sure to ASPIRE to all you can possibly become. Do not hesitate to reach for sublime happiness, great success, and wonderful relationships.

We are nothing if not realistic, which is critical to this journey. Just because you are divorced, that does not mean you can create a life that does not align with your talents, circumstances, finances, and so forth. If you cannot sing, you are not going to become the next great pop sensation. If you have no sense of timing, you are not going to become a stand-up comedian. If you are fifty years old and have always worked in the restaurant business, going to medical school is probably not a practical goal.

The key here is to identify the things that matter most to you, based on your abilities and available resources. If you have indeed worked in the restaurant business, maybe it is time for you to own your own place. If you live in New York and have always wanted to create a life in Florida, it could be time to figure out how to make that move. As Anthony Robbins often says, emotion begins with motion, and it's time for you to get moving.

Here are some questions, the answers to which you should be put in writing in your journal. Ask yourself…

> What do you want to do for a living—do you want to continue your current career or do you want to make a change? Have you left the work force and now want to return? Whatever your situation, THINK BIG.
>
> Assess your talents and strengths, identify what interests you, then GO FOR IT! Sit down and write a resume and be sure to include additional skills you gained in your marriage, especially things that went into child organization and management. Relate it all to what you think the position you are applying for might value. While you are at it, do not overlook your social relationships, new and old, to help find you an improved work position or even a new career.

What pursuits, beyond work, interest you? Do you want to travel? Learn a foreign language? Learn to play a musical instrument? Write a book? Join the church choir? Volunteer at your local hospital, help children in crisis, or work with wounded veterans? Paint? Quilt? Parachute out of a plane, learn to deep sea dive, work with dolphins, whales, or wild animals? Remember, you are free now. Create the life you want.

What about joining professional associations, going to workshops and attending conferences? There's no better way to get off that couch than to make plans and put them on your calendar.

Do you have a "bucket list" as we suggested earlier? If not, create one, with all the things you want to do and places you want to see, rediscovering old interests and exploring new horizons. Even if you do not get to all of them, it will be fun trying!

As you think about creating your new life, imagine that there are no limits—a great place to start. Limiting beliefs prevent us from becoming who we truly are. They will undercut your efforts to identify new opportunities and go after them. Stop worrying about what might go wrong or what might not happen. WHERE THE HELL DID DOUBT EVER GET YOU? If you hear voices telling you why your dreams are impossible, whether they come from outside or within, tell them to SHUT UP and then keep moving forward on your path to happiness, accomplishment, and love.

9.2 Finding someone to share the journey.

Finding a new relationship is only part of creating your new life—but it is undeniably an important part. We have already examined loneliness and how the fear of going through life without a partner causes some people to avoid divorce and remain in unhappy marriages.

But there is no reason to be alone.

Dating after divorce can feel like stepping into tumultuous and uncharted territory.

Having made the journey to Splitsville, you are facing a new world, loaded with excitement and fear and concerns about what lies ahead. Depending how long you have been married, entering the dating scene now may seem like learning a new computer program. Different rules, different methods, different devices.

We are often asked when it is best to start this process and how you will know you are ready? Believe us…

YOU ARE READY NOW!

You have worked hard throughout this book to identify what went wrong in your marriage. You have been introspective, honest with yourself and aware of what you want and what you do not.

Put those answers to good use, get off the couch and get out there. Start by meeting with friends for dinner or drinks or wherever you can comfortably gather. Let them know you are prepared to meet new people. That should be an easy first move.

Next steps may be more difficult, but you need to take them. Dating sites geared to your age are all over the Internet. Gatherings for singles are likely available at your place of worship and local community center. You should also find groups that engage in activities you enjoy—there is no better way to meet someone you will connect with than by doing something you like to do.

There are many opportunities. Book clubs. Theatre groups. Museum groups. Classes at a local college are offered to adults in many different subjects you will likely find intriguing. If it comes down to it, do not sit alone and watch a ballgame or Hallmark movie. Grab a friend and head to a local pub if necessary.

As you enter the dating process, continue to prioritize what you are looking for in a new relationship. Remember, you are the prize for someone to meet. Do not operate from fear of being rejected. Think of yourself as interviewing people rather than focusing on how you think they feel about you. Be patient as you work your way through new acquaintances and as you find your way. Do not become discouraged if it takes you a while to feel you have found the person that is right for you.

Eventually, you will find that spark of attraction toward a new romantic interest in your life. Just trust your instincts. They will be your most important asset. Use them to tune into the way a new person makes you feel. Trust what your gut is telling you. You have gotten in touch with who you are and your intuitive feelings will be your best guide.

Just a few tips to help guide you on this new path:

Patience

Patience is critical when you start dating, from finding the right person right up to sexual intimacy. If you give things time, you will feel more relaxed as you meet new people and be the best version of yourself.

Love yourself first

When you begin dating you may find yourself grasping for the romantic love you lost in your marriage. Just remember, true love can only exist if you love yourself first. You can only feel from another person what you first feel about yourself.

Be authentic

It may sound obvious to say this, but BE YOURSELF. How else can you build a new relationship? Many people tell us that they have difficulty accepting that who they are is fine and that it is wrong to try to be "more" or different than your true underlying being. Accepting yourself as you are is important, your goal is not to become a "different person," but to Be Yourself. If you feel you are having trouble relaxing about who you truly are, it may be a red flag that you are not dating the right person. If you are "faking something," the chances are good that you do not feel the person you are dating will truly like you for yourself. Take a deep breath and MOVE ON.

Avoid comparisons

We admit this is often difficult, since there is a natural tendency to compare your new relationship with others you are meeting or—worst of all—your former spouse. Think how unfair this is to the new person in your life. Accept everyone for who he or she is and make your decisions based on that.

Do not confuse need with affection

You do not want your new relationship becoming bogged down with need. Stay loose, as the saying goes. Being yourself will help with that. While it is normal for couples who are newly dating to spend a good deal of their free time together, avoid behavior that becomes too demanding or restricting—for either of you.

Continue spending time with family and old friends

You might feel so invested in establishing a new relationship that you may find you are spending less and less time on your usual activities and those who are already a part of your life. This is trouble on many levels, the most important of which is this—do not lose your true identity in a new relationship.

Trust your instincts

We hope on your journey to Splitsville, you have confronted a lot about yourself. Trust what you have learned! Too often, in post-divorce dating, there is a tendency to ignore what should be clear about the new person. As you get caught up in a new romance, do not forget what you have discovered about you, about your needs, and your aspirations. Do not hesitate to go back and review your responses to our questionnaires and be careful you are not rationalizing what may be clear signs of negative behavior you should not accept. We are not suggesting you become overly critical, but you have worked hard to get to this position of freedom and self- awareness ... TRUST YOUR INSTINCTS.

9.3 Children and dating

If you still have children living with you, they will have to be factored into your dating life and the forming of a new relationship. Most psychologists suggest that you should know your new relationship about six months before you introduce him/her to your children and the rest of your family. Introducing children before you are sure you are making him/her a permanent relationship can be stressful for them. Wait until you find someone you feel is special to you. Even if you are sure that your new relationship is going to be serious, you still want to go slow involving the children. When the time comes to make the introduction, involve them in activities they will find enjoyable, but do not suddenly include your new partner in everything you do with the children. It should be a gradual progression. No matter how close you are becoming in your new relationship, you must stress to the children that they will always come first.

In the final analysis, this is your life and as long as you are sensitive to the feelings of your children, move ahead.

9.4 Getting your sh*t together

You want to start dating as part of your new life, you know you do. But you have issues. You have allowed yourself to get out of shape. Perhaps you think your teeth are the color of corn on the cob. Or you see yourself as too heavy or too thin. You need to restyle your hair, upgrade your wardrobe, get a manicure, a pedicure, a facial. Whatever you feel you need, take action!

The excuses abound, but whatever the truth is for you, you know what it is! You know what you need to do, so do it! Get off the couch, take a long look in the mirror and make an honest assessment, and then be sure to take some action steps. It does not have to be difficult or expensive. Just get your hand out of that bag of potato chips and begin by doing some sit-ups, push-ups and jumping jacks. Whatever it takes, start the process. Do NOT just think or plan or imagine—you must act, and you must do it right away.

And, by the way, do not compare yourself to fashion models, movie stars, professional athletes, and people twenty years your junior. Do not try to convince yourself of the impossibility of the tasks ahead. You are who you are, which is simply wonderful. Now get it together and maximize your assets so you feel good about yourself as you make your way to happiness.

9.5 You have passed through Splitsville and there is happiness ahead.

You have survived one of life's most challenging experiences. It is not just your marital status that has changed—your life has shifted. Very few are prepared for what it feels like to be divorced. For many, it is particularly difficult to transition to the solo life. So, what are you going to do about it? Mope? Complain? Give up your aspirations for a happy future?

If you have traveled this far with us, we know that is not true. You may feel as if your life has been turned upside down, but you are going to pursue your dreams and make the best of what lies ahead. Right? That is certainly what we want for you.

It may take some time to become accustomed to your new status—some research suggests it can take a year or two—but it really is up to *you.* There will be ups and downs along the way, but do not give in to the "downs." Not only do you want happiness, you deserve it, and to that end we have a few observations and anecdotes to share.

If you think you need it, arrange for professional help and support

You may have friends who will permit you to sob on their shoulders and sleep on their couch when you cannot face being alone, but resist indulging in that sort of a pity party. As pointed out in our chapter on selecting a counselor, a professional will help you cope and provide guidance as you figure out how to jump-start your new life.

Keep a journal

People who write about what is disturbing them tend to show a significant improvement in mood, overall feeling, things being good, and hopefulness. Journaling, or you may call it writing about your emotional struggles, reduces anxiety and pain.

Keeping a journal helped people with post-traumatic stress disorder, according to a 2008 Syracuse University study. Participants wrote either about their distress or a neutral topic for three months. Those who wrote about disturbing experiences showed a significant improvement in their moods and responses to memories of what happened. We encourage you to keep a journal and every few days write about your feelings. Journaling can give you a comparison to where you were, where you are now, and can help to inspire you.

If you need to grieve, do it, then cut it out

We have pointed out that grieving is natural when going through a divorce. The splitting up of your marriage is in some ways similar to a death and it's natural to mourn what you have lost, even if you were the one who wanted to split. So, make time to grieve if you must. Let the sadness come and go and then get past it. You have a new life to live!

Make new friends

We have already said not to abandon old friends, your family and things you enjoy. However, we frequently hear divorced people complain that their old friends no longer seem to invite them out as a single person. In some instances, those friends enjoyed both the husband and wife as a couple, but they might feel threatened by the fact that you are single and perhaps a threat to their own marriage. Whatever the reason, your group of friends may shrink a bit, but the world is open to you to make new friends, perhaps from different walks of life. Perhaps people from new and varied backgrounds.

As a single person, you are in a different social pool. As we said earlier, pursue those who share your interests and be sure to include new *single* friends. Your common situation will create an easy bond.

Your finances are now *your* finances

Financial independence is one of the most important components of your life after divorce. Regardless of the arrangements you made with your former spouse regarding the divorce, it is highly recommended that you do whatever is necessary to gain a state of financial self-reliance. If you were not working, it may mean getting a job, at least part-time, which will not only bring in some money, but will also give you another avenue for meeting new people. Remember that you can do whatever you want, there is no longer a spouse to intervene, pass judgment or to stop you from living your dreams.

GIVE YOURSELF CREDIT—

YOU GOT DIVORCED. CELEBRATE YOUR FREEDOM!

You have made it to Splitsville and you have arrived in one piece, physically and emotionally. So, CELEBRATE! Take a trip with friends, old or new, or with your children. You do not need to spend a fortune, just get in the car if necessary and go someplace fun. Several people we know have thrown a "divorce shower" after the gavel came down and they were free. It is a wonderful way for everyone to see that you are all right, you have emerged from the turmoil a stronger person and are ready to go on to a new life.

We hope we have made your journey to Splitsville less stressful, less expensive, and more enlightened, and have set you on the road ahead that will be lined with happiness and love.

ACKNOWLEDGMENTS

We want to acknowledge the numerous scholarly works and studies we have reviewed in writing this book, and encourage you, if you are interested, to do further reading on your own:

Kristin Celello, a Professor of History and the Director of American Studies at Queens College, is the author of *Making Marriage Work: A History of Marriage and Divorce in The Twentieth-Century United States.*

Stephanie Coontz, author of *Marriage, a History: How Love Conquered Marriage* (Penguin books, 2006)

Godbeer, author of *Sexual Revolution in Early America* (JHUP, 2004)

Attachment theory, by Ainsworth and John Bowlby

Hazan and Shaver, of the Institute for Family Studies, author of "Who Cheats More? The Demographics of Infidelity in America." Jan. 10, 2018)

Knopp K, Scott S, Ritchie L, Rhoades GK, Markman HJ, Stanley SM. Once a Cheater, Always a Cheater? Serial Infidelity Across Subsequent Relationships. Arch Sex Behav. 2017; 46(8):2301-2311.

"The State of Affairs: Rethinking Infidelity" by Esther Perel

"Healing from Infidelity" by Michele Weiner-Davis

Couple Family Psychol., C.A. Johnson, 2001 Author manuscript; available in PMC 2014 Jun 1. 2013, 2(20 131-145)

Couple Family Psychol., C.A. Johnson, 2001 Author manuscript; available in PMC 2014 Jun 1. A study performed and published in Couple family Psychology, 2013, 2(20 131-145.

Couple Family Psychol., C.A. Johnson, 2001 Author manuscript; available in PMC 2014 Jun 1.2013, 2(20 131-145

John Gottman, the theory of "contempt"

Charmetski, C., and Brennan, F. published their research in 2004 in PubMed in an article termed Sexual Frequency and Salivary Immunoglobulin, which unquestionably showed that people who had sex "more frequently," definitely had better immune systems.

Hall, S., and Shackleton, M.S., published a research study in the American Journal of Cardiology, in January, 2010, showing that that having regular sex may reduce the risk of developing heart disease.

Kravdal, Q., Gundy, E., Children's age at parental divorce and depression in early and mid-adulthood, Population Studies: A Journal of Demography, vol. 73, (1) 2019

Journal of marriage and Family, April 2015, The Production of Inequality: The Gender Division of Labor Across the Transition to Parenthood, J. E., Yavorsky, C.M., Dush & S. S., Sullivan

ABOUT THE AUTHORS

JEFFREY S. STEPHENS

A native of New York City, the author is a successful attorney in private practice, having handled many divorces and family law issues, both in New York and Connecticut. Stephens has lived for more than thirty years in Greenwich, which is where he and his wife Nancy raised their two sons, Graham and Trevor. Stephens is the author of the Jordan Sandor thrillers, *Targets of Deception, Targets of Opportunity, Targets of Revenge* and *Rogue Mission*, as well as the Anthony Walker murder mystery *Crimes and Passion* and the Pencraft First Place Award winning novel, *Fool's Errand.* Stephens newest novel is the just released thriller *The Handler* from Post Hill Press.

DR. RONALD RAYMOND

A clinical psychologist who has been practicing for over fifty years, his background includes time as a professor and adjunct professor at several universities. He served as the Director of Psychology at one of the Nation's most prestigious psychiatric hospitals, Silver Hill Hospital in New Canaan, CT, and was the developer of Transition, Inc., where he had the opportunity to counsel, in group fashion, over 5000 prospective corporate transferring families. He was also in charge of Relocation Counselor training for IBM, a consultant regarding transferring families to General Electric, General Foods, Merck, General Motors and many other Fortune 500 Corporations, and the exclusive consultant to Home Equity, the leading relocation management company in the U. S. The American Psychological Association attributed, to him, the development of the branch of relocation psychology. Through his involvement with relocation for many corporations, he coauthored the book *Grow Your Roots Anywhere, Anytime.* In private practice, Dr. Raymond has counseled children and adults, including many going through the issues of divorce. He is also the coauthor of *Ring of Destiny, and the author of Destiny Revealed* and *The Four Essential Ingredients for Effective Parenting.*

Made in United States
North Haven, CT
27 March 2023